Psychic Profiler

The Real Deal

True Crime Cases

Vol. 1

Robbie Thomas

ISBN: 1984986244
ISBN-13: 978-1984986245

Psychic Profiler The Real Deal

For My Wife Ligia
I Love You!

You have been my confidant, friend, and the strength I've needed over our marriage, through what we both have called, 'the good, the bad and the ugly', of what it is I do. You have been there through it all, coming on death scenes with me, to family's homes during their crises, and sitting in office with Law Enforcement, being my shoulder to lean on. You have seen much, witnessing the variables I go through on each case presented and never once have you wavered in being you…my beautiful wife.

You my dear truly are a blessing in disguise!

I thank the Lord above every day for you and I know I wouldn't have been able to do what it is I do day in and day out if it weren't for you.

Thank You…

I Love You Dearly!

Table Of Contents

Psychic Profiler The Real Deal

Endorsement For Robbie Thomas

I have been extremely blessed to have been introduced to Robbie Thomas, and have maintained a lasting relationship with him since. Other endorsements may label him "The Real Deal", but that's not even in question here. The importance of what Robbie is able to do is monumental. What he does, brings healing, closure (be it good or bad), compassion, and hope to those who are grieving. For a family missing a loved one, the not knowing is the worse part. Law enforcement has limited capabilities, must work within strict guidelines, and often is overwhelmed. However, using unconventional methods and gifts such as Robbie possesses, evil can and will be conquered! Families will be reunited, order restored and relief for the grieving. We all owe Robbie a debt of gratitude for the work he has done, the toll it has taken on him. But as gracious and humble as he is, he will never ask for it. So I will. Read the book, keep an open mind, and delve into the world of a genuine psychic profiler.

Lt. Kevin Thompson
Team 2 Shift commander
Madison County Sheriff Department
Madison County, Alabama
Military Police Instructor, 1st Bn 200th RTI

Law Enforcement Perspective On Robbie Thomas

"Psychic Profiler The Real Deal" is a truly amazing book based on a few of the multitude of cases handled by Robbie Thomas, Psychic Criminal Profiler. It dwells deep into the cases he's handled, showing step by step, how his amazing talent/gift works. It goes into the darkest of realms, into the minds of monsters, viewing through the eyes of victims, and shows how his gift works from beginning to end. It shows the emotional side of Robbie and sometimes the strain it takes to decipher what he's seeing. With documentation of cases, letters, text messages, Detective testimonials as well as Law Enforcement and families stepping up to endorse him, it demonstrates with validity how he helps those families cope with the horrors they've been through. No matter the outcome, Good or bad, Robbie is there as a beacon of strength to all. As an Officer of the law, who has worked with Robbie extensively, I can say he is truly an amazing person and this is an amazing book and reflection of who he is.

Det. Sgt. Cliff Christ
Retired Police Officer, Colorado

Authors note

Throughout the many years of assisting Law Enforcement and families when they have requested my help, my life, my normalcy of anything less, than being someone everyone turns to, in order to find some sense of rational from some of the most heinous crimes, has taken a back seat for the most part. I don't mean anything bad by this, it's something I've actually reflected upon many times, wondering, what if, I was just a normal Joe in some sense, where there wasn't any of this whatsoever? Oh yes, it has and does cross my mind at times, more in the later part of my life where I'm trying to find the rest of my life so-to-speak.

I don't want to sound rash or redundant in any respect, I'm just being me, just a guy who long ago was full of insight and wanting to help out as much as possible, without the many roadblocks that followed that good-fellow. It hasn't been a smooth ride whatsoever throughout my life, but it has been a ride most certainly.

Nothing in life comes easy for anyone and with that said; I can assure you, it hasn't for me at all as well. Some think, just because you have sight, ability, gift from God, or whatever you wish to think it might be called or labeled, what I can say is, regardless of what others think, say or feel, it's my life and I choose to do what I feel on how I utilize the ability I have.

There will always be that one individual or individuals, who will have something opposite to say in life of anything anyone does because of the fact they aren't in control of what that person possesses or are not quite understanding of it. In hindsight, you can't please everyone in life and there's nothing wrong with that. As long as you, do what you feel is good in your heart and soul, this is what really matters in life and the only thing that matters.

To the skeptics out there, who are about to read this body of work, pertaining to my life, I totally get it; I really do and in some sense, really appreciate you. Everyone has the right to think what they will, which isn't a bad thing; it's actually invited to a certain degree. That degree is being able to use a common sense approach, realizing the proof within the pages that are literally documented throughout and recognizing the truth when you see it. Hence, "The writing is on the wall!" No one is bashing anyone in what you read here now, nor, will there be any in the future. I don't fear, or worry whatsoever, what one might try to do to discredit what is in black and white, straight forward within these pages, which are illustrated throughout the documentation, validation, testimonials and more. Only they, who try to find some discrepancy, regardless of the facts, are the ones who go beyond that common sense of reality, crossing the line in trying to intimidate, which in turn, becomes only a bully crying because they can't get their own way. I have orchestrated a well put together piece of literature, which leaves nothing to chance, or wanting to just seem like it was some frivolous writing without careful consideration.

Psychic Profiler The Real Deal

These are the cases, which have occupied my life through being requested or demanded to help others unselfishly. In turn, I have the absolute right in every context of this meaning, to write about my life, my involvement, and circumstances that involved me in cases that this book offers for everyone to see. It isn't taking advantage of anyone and those who try to step up to say different, remember, look within the pages before you do, the testimonial letters are from the families and Law Enforcement themselves. People have the right to know, the right to know who is actively out there, assisting Law Enforcement, Agencies and families without discourse or hate towards the messenger. Now, please, sit back and enjoy a good read with Psychic Profiler –The Real Deal.

Thank you!

More Endorsements

President Of Crime Stoppers Sarnia, Sean Robbins, shakes Robbie's hand in supporting each other in the fight against crime and the betterment of our community.

"Crime Stoppers are pleased to endorse and work long side Robbie Thomas, as he's a huge supporter of Crime Stoppers in the endeavor, to fight crime and keep our community safe."

- Sean Robbins, President, Crime Stoppers, Sarnia, Ontario

Psychic Profiler The Real Deal

"As a Peace Officer "The real deal", "a true psychic", are terms we use to describe the surprise gift we find in Robbie Thomas. For me, he must be respected and utilized when his information is offered. A witness is someone who sees what you didn't or can't and that information may be necessary to advance the case. In any serious crime investigation all tips must be followed up, no matter what your personal belief system. Opening your mind to Robbie, may save a life or reunite loved ones and if you judge someone's investigational skill by their track record, then common sense says that his gift must be able to assist. We no longer have to fear ridicule for the assistance of psychics, it's well documented that they can help."

- Cpl. James Tyson, Royal Canadian Mounted Police. (R.C.M.P.)

"I have worked with Robbie Thomas first hand as an active Law Enforcement Officer. Robbie's gift coupled with good police work gives victims and families closure and puts bad guys in jail. Thank God that you have chosen to use your gift to help those who need you! In Law Enforcement, we regularly use K-9's to track down criminals who have just committed a crime. We use you, along with your gift, to track down those who have committed the worst of atrocities...That no K-9 could ever track. Thank you, Robbie!" - Law Enforcement Officer, Andy DeLay, Florida

"I feel fortunate to have been able to read about Robbie Thomas, because he is the "Real Deal." I've known him for a number of years and have even discussed one of my former cases with him.

Thomas pours a lot of himself into cases where he's helped assist individuals and the police. I have great respect for Thomas and his dedication to helping the families who become the victims of unsolved murders and missing persons. It's been interesting reading about where he comes from and what's made him into the person he is today. It's a fascinating trip into the mind of Thomas and a few of his many cases. Whether you're interested in the psychic that he is or the aspect of the crimes he's helped solve, you won't be disappointed. I know I wasn't and I know him!" - Martha Decker, Retired Assistant Chief of Police, Tool PD

"The arrests were made, exactly how you said it would happen! It was just amazing! I don't endorse Psychics at all, but Robbie Thomas is one I totally stand behind." - Retired International Police Chief, Kevin Smith, United States

"Very powerful stuff, Robbie Thomas has skills that most Police Officers could only dream of. He is the REAL DEAL!" - Sgt. Cliff Christ, Retired Police Investigator, Colorado

Acknowledgements

I want to express my heartfelt love, to all the families I've had the opportunity to help over the many years, during your time of need with your loved one's murder or missing person's cases. I know there are no words that can express or take away your pain, I know also, there's nothing no one can do to bring back the normality in your lives, however, I do know my love for you all is strong and I'm here to help always. I continually think and pray for all of you, in hopes that one day the pain in your hearts will diminish just a little more than it was the day before. May God Bless you all and give you peace you so deserve.

With much love in my heart for my family, you are my pillar, my rock that I fall upon, which carries me to the next day. My gratitude for everything you have done, to show the support, not only for me, but for all those families you put yourself aside for, in order for me to assist them for days, weeks, and months at a time. I love you dearly! Because you understand and have understood, the painstaking amount of time away from you meant so much for people we didn't even know…I know we call them, "Perfect Strangers", and it has great meaning to us, as they've become part of our family in a special way.

I love you so much! I know by giving up so much in our lives for others, we grow stronger for each other in our lives. Many people don't realize the sacrifice, you, my darling family has given, in order to assist many other families internationally, but my heart so honors you for this. Love you forever and more.

To all Law Enforcement, Specialists, many different agencies and organizations, who have believed in me and allowing me to work alongside you, in order to find that one missing clue or piece of evidence, you're remarkable without a doubt. God Bless The Blue Line and the extraordinary teams of people, who have crossed my life in order to help those in their time of need! There aren't enough words to express the valor or selfless acts of kindness you all show, day in and day out for people who need your outstretched hand. I applaud you and give you my total support in life always. To my fans, all of you, who have followed me from early on in my life's work; from the mid-nineties up until now, thank you for being so supportive in every aspect of my life.

Thank You, for coming from far and wide to events to see me, watching news broadcasts of me discussing cases, reading all my books, watching my movies and just cheering me on, in hopes that we find resolve to a case of a missing person or a murder case that is or seemed very difficult to solve, you've touched my heart.

Those of you out there, who I haven't had the opportunity to meet, but still stay vigilant in following me on social media, God Bless You and God Bless Everyone. I feel your great intentions and your goodwill always from the messages, emails, and posting you send me on a daily basis.

Much love to you all…

About The Author

Robbie Thomas is a Psychic Medium/Spiritual Counselor, who helps internationally, families and Police, fight against crime while bringing solace to those who need it. Over many years of assisting in many murder/missing person's cases, Robbie has been able to give great details to these devastating crimes or happenings, which have led to finding lost people, arrests being made in murder cases, and bringing closure to families who desperately need it. Robbie works closely with families in conjunction with Law Enforcement. Being highly respected in both the Paranormal/Spiritual fields of work, Robbie continues to be a great presence, working alongside many integral individuals in Film, Television, and Radio, lending his ability furthering along, his experience as a Spiritual Visionary. Robbie lives in Canada and is often called upon from the international community for assistance with his ability. Being a prolific Author/Writer in the Metaphysical/Spiritual, Horror/Paranormal genre's, he's published eight books of his own and co-contributed to four other books. He's written television treatments, which have been looked at and has accomplished one of them to be in development. Other projects of Robbie's have also been given consideration with other production companies (United States and Canada).

Movies have also been a part of Robbie's life as he has either created or starred in, Dead Whisper 2005-2006, The Sallie House 2007, and Paradox (Parasylum Directors Cut 2009). Robbie has been seen on one-hour television specials and news media, NBC, CBS, ABC, GAIA TV, CKCO, Daytime Live Rogers Television, StarChoice, Bell Expressview, New RO (CTV), and many other television programs. He's been featured on, CBS Radio, ZTalk Radio, Kevin Smith Show, Barbara Mackey Show CBS, True Ghost Stories Show, Keeler Show New York, Bob FM, The Eagle 103.3 FM, CHOK 1070 AM, The Fox 99.9 and more. He has been featured in many magazines worldwide such as Taps Paranormal Magazine (United States), Intrepid Magazine (United States), Visions Magazine (United States), Signs Magazine (England), Bellesprit Magazine (United States), Suspense Magazine (United States), Paranormal Magazine (England), Unexplained Paranormal Magazine (United States), Fix Magazine (Canada), Pen It Magazine (United States) and more.

Foreword #1

Asst. Chief Of Police, Martha D~~~~~

Robbie Thomas is a person I've known for a number of years and while getting to know him a little bit through social media, I received a phone call from him about an unsolved case in Texas. It was an unsolved murder that had long gone cold, which needed to be looked at once more. This is a specialty of Robbie's, as we still hope to investigate it further together in the future and possibly even help solve the case for the victim's family. Robbie pours a lot of himself into cases where he's helped assist individuals and the police for decades. Lucky for Robbie, he has an understanding wife who chose to support him as he wanders his chosen path in finding justice for victims' families and those who go missing.

We talk often and have run into each other at paranormal conferences, where either I am speaking or Robbie is speaking on the work he does with Law Enforcement. I have spoken at conferences about how to take the forensic interview into interviewing witnesses and clients in the paranormal world for several years, transforming the utilization of techniques. My work in this field cranked up on retirement day. It can be difficult to sit on the witness stand, during a felony case, only to have a defense attorney try to discredit you as a credible person using any paranormal information they find, albeit legitimate or not.

Robbie nearly became a police officer and in my opinion, would have been good at the job. That's my true gut feeling as former law enforcement myself. It's your gut that helps keep you alive as an officer in the line of duty and it never leaves you that instinct. It also helps ferret out criminals, and can help you discern who is lying, or telling the truth. Of course, spending years learning to profile individuals, through watching for changes in demeanor, and finding their "tells" helps efficiently in cases.

I had a case involving the murder of a 12 year old before retiring from law enforcement and it was the first time the police department used the Texas Aber Alert. We got calls from all over the place. Vetting the calls was tough for a small department at the time making the task very difficult. While I have my suspicions, I retired from my position in Law Enforcement without solving the case. That case sits in the back of my mind and often on the tip of my tongue. It could be about drugs or money, but it was not good either way. As if murder is ever good. The alleged suspect, in my mind is sitting in prison now for another felony that was committed before the murder of the 12 year old. There are so many red flags on this case as Robbie and I have discussed it many times and even though I'm now retired, it's my hope that we will see the case through, having it solved sooner than later. Some individuals might have the belief that a psychic shouldn't know anything about a case because it could influence the input they receive. While that is partially true, being aware of some information and being able to visualize can help with information received tremendously.

Psychic Profiler The Real Deal

There are some psychics who will brag about solving the crime with no information detailing their involvement.

While that is great, where is the information and what was the case, detective on that case etc.? I could be called the open minded skeptic; however, if detectives keep an open mind, they may find help from outside their ring of information. Now, that doesn't mean that everyone who claims to be "psychic" should pick up the phone and bombard law enforcement with information not proven to be credible. Robbie has worked many years forming bonds with detectives and word of mouth gets him calls from detectives he has yet to meet. At least that is my opinion. Take it for what it's worth.

Robbie and I are working together on a case of murder in a different state at present. As it gets solved, there will be some very surprised individuals looking on. When I first started getting information that Robbie received through the mail and email about the case, there were so many red flags as to whom, how, and possibly, why this murder was committed. A cop chalks it up to gut feelings and years of experience looking at everything from many angles.

It's funny when we discuss the matter at hand every few weeks, we both have drawn the same conclusions on almost every aspect of the case. All of this without communicating beforehand, which makes it much more credible from an investigating stand point. Robbie taking it in through the eyes of a psychic profiler, where my eyes still see it as though I'm a detective. It works well when the law and the psychic see through the same eyes, yet independently, but on the same page coming to a solid conclusion.

I have great respect for Robbie for his dedication in helping the families who have become victims of unsolved murders and missing persons, like the missing or murdered or even those sold into human trafficking. There are so many missing people left alone and lost at some unknown location, living in fear, scared and or deceased.

Robbie has become an advocate for those who have been trafficked in this horrible trade. I did the same while working for the State of Texas and was part of an anti-human trafficking task force. Many people assume that this is something that happens overseas, in Europe, or third world countries. It happens often in the United States, Canada, and right in our own back yards. There were 10 federal multi-disciplinary human trafficking tasks forces with three or four of them being in Texas. This is the state where I reside and had my career in Law Enforcement. It isn't just sex slaves; it also encompasses labor slaves and much more. The fact Robbie assisting in this type of case will make a difference for some of the missing, as he is dedicated in finding justice for all.

Then there are those individuals who have chosen to disappear. Yes, Robbie has even located living individuals who have gone missing for great lengths at a time or short periods of time. This can also give families much needed peace of mind even though the missing person chose to disconnect from family and friends. I am sure there are other missing person cases, which may be individuals choosing to go away from their life and start fresh, falling off the map so to speak. Who hasn't had that thought at least once in their life? It beats out other ways to disappear.

Psychic Profiler The Real Deal

Robbie has had death threats, stalkers, hate mail and other not so nice communication often from suspects or trolls. They hear he is involved and become afraid he will out them, which is his purpose. That could be an interesting form of evidence that he is getting too close to solving a case. Many would choose to walk away. Not Robbie, he will walk straight toward the danger to help victims, their families, and law enforcement without blinking an eye. It seems to be engrained in his DNA.

Robbie's newest book delves into his mind, so we can see how he ticks when working a case. Once you read the book you'll think you've known him for a bit longer than you thought. If you like reading about unsolved cases and how they become solved, then this book is for you. If you're psychic and are unsure of what to do, if you think you have knowledge of a crime, then this book can help you understand the process in which it is or how one should take. Learn what he did, grasp from someone who is a great teacher in his own right. Robbie writes about how he started interacting with law enforcement many years ago and why he chose to step out of an opportunity to be an officer. The book may also open the eyes of the doubter in law enforcement that, yes, some psychics really do work with police on a continuous basis.

Martha Hazzard Decker,
Retired Assistant Chief of Police/Detective
Tool Texas PD
Retired Special Investigator for State of Texas
Author of Paranormal Profiling

Foreword #2

President Crime Stopper, Sean Robbins

Growing up as teenagers, literally a block away from each other, both Robbie and I were friends and have continued throughout life. It's in the establishment of our friendship that credibility has formed its foundation for both of us and of who he is. Now, later in life, our directions continually cross for the involvement in the desire to help our community. It's in this desire we both share that our friendship has grown into a professional aspect, working with Law Enforcement and finding resolve to crimes committed by criminals. Mine is being the President of Crime Stoppers in Sarnia, Ontario, Canada and serving this community for the betterment of all and Robbie has elevated his ability to assist many communities throughout the world.

Knowing of his "ability", the capable way he lends himself to assist many levels of Law Enforcement and Agencies, Robbie's work is impeccable; becoming a most sought after asset in helping to solve some of the most heinous crimes known. This book only illustrates the absolute in truth, with much factual element to each case within its pages. The uncanny way in piecing together some of the hardest, intricate dispositions needed to find the next level of investigation, or even wrapping up a case in a matter of hours, days, or weeks is something of a phenomenon.

Psychic Profiler The Real Deal

Crime in any sense in our society has no place whatsoever; it's through the dedication of many men and women on the front lines of Law Enforcement in whom we trust that make that impact and difference. They put their lives on the line each and every day for our communities to protect and serve, and in saying this, they have entrusted the assistance from Robbie Thomas at various times over the many years. Within this body of work by this Author, are those entrusted, dedicated, testimonials, which establish without a doubt, an undisputed brotherhood that has been forged in friendship over the many years. Facts are what is needed in verifying any credibility in life of a professional in his/her career and who they are. The facts that are documented in a remarkable way in this book, is without a doubt, the credibility of a Psychic Medium with true ability and service to the people. Lastly in saying, those of you who pick up this book; will ultimately not want to put it down and only wish there were more to read. It is enticing, intriguing, and inexplicably engulfing! Walking through each case and being drawn in like you were right there on scene with Robbie, is an extraordinary accomplishment of a true visionary. Putting to words from start to finish, cases of murder, missing person's and a medical mystery, showing complete knowledge through sight, prayer or mysteries of the universe, is something in itself credible! A friend that has established who he is and formed a lasting impression on me with all he does.

Sean Robbins

President

Crime Stoppers, Sarnia Ontario, Canada

How It All Began

At age seventeen, I wanted to become one of the blue line members, so I started my pursuit of becoming a police officer in my hometown. I was resourceful while beginning my research, in what was needed for schooling and what was expected from someone who wanted to become a police officer. I looked up the finest colleges and universities in Ontario, Canada, however, couldn't make up my mind, as to which one was the best. My family & I knew the mayor of our city and he gave me some insight into whom to speak with on the Sarnia force. I placed a call, asking for the inspector as I was instructed, and we struck up quite the conversation about a career in law enforcement.

I explained that there was a great college in Hamilton, Ontario, I heard of, which had exceptional training and teaching for law. The inspector hinted to me that the force was actually taking three auxiliaries and testing would be in a couple weeks. He also stated that I would do better to do the testing and, if chosen, the schooling would be through the force, where they would send me to Aylmer Police College. Well, bells went off in my head, thoughts of grandeur and more, as I had my in and I'm not going to pass this up for anything.

I went into the station, noticing there were quite a few people doing testing at the time, as I peered around the room they had us in. I thought to myself, "I'm going to get this and no one is going to beat me, I want it bad!" I did all the written testing and waited.

Psychic Profiler The Real Deal

I kept looking at the clock on the wall, watching the time slip away while that one door opened and closed, as every prospected individual walked through it, hoping they were the one selected. I was one of the last called in and when they called my name, my blood pressure shot through the roof. Here it is, this is it, time for the truth, and that moment I've been waiting for. Walking across the threshold of that office, where two gentlemen sat in suits, detectives who ran the testing, they were looking over everyone's file and testing scores, which seemed a bit intimidating.

All I heard was "Have a seat!" My heart raced, watching in anticipation, waiting for the verdict of either they accepted me or not. The one detective looked up at me saying, "You scored in the top three on all the written testing, good for you young man!" I now knew I was in and nothing was going to hold me back. I sat very calm, well, as calm as I could be, considering I just got told I was in the top three. My heart was pounding out of my chest and I'm certain these guys knew that; however, I was congratulated and told to follow the one detective along with the other two who were waiting, as we headed to the Chief of Police's Office down the hall.

As we sat in the office of the Chief, waiting for him to greet us, you could hear this burly guys voice, coming closer to the door and making his way in. He smiled at us all, but had his eye on me as he took his seat in the office. He congratulated the other two auxiliaries sitting there and then, turned to me, with a huge grin on his face. See, to be an auxiliary, one has to obtain the age of at least twenty years of age.

Well, I didn't know that and I really didn't care because hey, I made it right? I beat out all those other candidates, and that's all that matters. Funny that, it doesn't work that way in the real world, and I found out as he began to laugh, explaining to me what the protocol was of becoming an officer. "Son", he said, "How old are you?" I looked at the other two sitting there as they just glared at me, wondering what was going on. See, I had a mustache and was built like a twenty year old, so I guess I passed the look, but my age, it seemed to get the better of me. I answered back to the Chief, "I'm seventeen, Sir!" The other two laughed out loud and the Chief laughed as well.

He reassured me it wasn't anything bad or he didn't think anything wrong about what had just happened, but he couldn't get over a seventeen year old beating out all the other prospects. He looked at me and said, "This will be a day you'll most likely remember forever. You were hired and fired in the same day!" He then explained to me, to come back when I was twenty to try again, but in the meantime, why don't I try college and take a law course. Doesn't that beat all! That's what my first intentions were. I thought to myself, "I can always say that I was a cop, for a minute anyway!"

Looking back at this experience, I knew there was much more for me to do and to follow my dreams. I mean, this was it, this is exactly what I wanted to do with my life; therefore, I'm pushing fast forward on the acceleration button, to become the ripe old age of twenty and start once more. I had my sight on the prize, and couldn't wait for my next round of testing, so, I buried the thoughts of the hire and fire episode quickly and anticipated my next venture.

Psychic Profiler The Real Deal

Here I am, age twenty, looking at the mountains of research I've done in finding out all the centers that were conducting police testing, and taking on new recruits. I started to make new friends at it, and it seemed there was a circuit of testing every other week in a different city or town across Ontario. I went through quite a few, making it to the final interviews, only to be told that one day I would indeed make a great police officer, but not today. The crushing blows kept coming and I was getting burnt out from it all and of course, being told that same old line, that one day, but when was that one day coming?

Finally, I'm in a center just outside of Toronto, Canada, breezing through all the physical testing, written testing and the psychological testing. Now, I come to the long line of multiple interviews, which seem to be the make or break you epilogue to everything that was conducted for the long weekend of tests. They told us before the last interview that, if we made it this far and at the end of our one on one with the final interviewer, we'd know if we were chosen. I had high anticipation, nerves that kept me on edge and that darn clock in the waiting room, tick-tock, tick-tock, oh how I dreaded that clock.

The door opened for the last time as I made my way in for the final interview. I sat in front of a sergeant who informed me, I was accepted and congratulations, welcome to the force. There were formalities of paperwork, a few loose ends to be tied up, but I would be coming back down to the city after next week for further induction and information.

I was elated and couldn't wait to get home to spread the good news. Part of the deal was we had to relocate to this new city; therefore, we had to give notice where we were living, give away our dog because of the home we were going to rent wouldn't allow dogs, but these things were minor as I realized in my heart, I'm finally going to become a Police Officer.

While being back home and given the good news, I was in the kitchen having coffee with my father who came over to hear my excitement. During our conversation, I heard a lady screaming at the top of her voice, "Accident…Accident, please help!" I opened my screen patio door to my backyard, raced over to the fence where I was met by a frantic elderly lady. I climbed over, noticing her pointing south, along the long driveway of the townhomes that were behind my home. I began to jog at a quick pace to the area in which she directed me to go and as I turned down the curve in the driveway that led towards the roadway, I noticed there wasn't any accident there and there wasn't anything happening whatsoever.

I turned, to see a man yelling, motioning me to come towards him at one of the townhomes, so I ran over and in doing so, he pulled me in by my shoulder. I stepped into a kitchen area, witnessing a woman running around a kitchen table, screaming and crying loudly to my left while another gentleman to my right was holding a doorknob to a door that led to another room. He was very pale, with his eyes wider than I've seen on anyone in a very long time. He had this look on his face as if he seen death or death was warmed all over him.

Psychic Profiler The Real Deal

I made my way to the gentleman and as soon as I did, he grabbed my arm, opened the door to the room he was guarding, shoves me in while I kept my eyes focused on the floor looking for blood because I was told, it was an accident from the first lady I had seen. My eyes were quickly greeted, by yet another gentleman, sitting on the toilet naked, staring right at me. His gaunt look with slight purple lips, indicated to me immediately that he either had a heart attack or he was not breathing at all. Well, both seemed to be right as I reached out to check his pulse, noticing he didn't have one. I checked once more to make sure while starting to talk to him, but his eyes told the entire story.

I could see, he just passed on and there wasn't anything anyone would be able to do. Regardless, of this feeling I had, I must start CPR as this was part of my training going through to be a police officer. As I go to start CPR, grabbing this gentleman to place him on the floor, a voice echoed in that bathroom. "Let me go!" Yes, that is exactly what I heard and my reaction you might ask? I stepped back for a brief moment, looking directly into his eyes and said, "What did you just say to me? Hello, I heard you!" Nothing, not a word and still cold, and clammy to the touch, so I go to start CPR once more and then, I hear louder this time, "LET ME GO!" That's it; this guy is not being touched by me again. He's really telling me to not touch him and to not administer CPR, loud and clear. I get it!

I exited that small interior bathroom, only to be greeted by at least a dozen people staring directly at me, waiting for some sign or answer to the wellbeing of the man I just left. You could hear a pin drop! It seemed like the world came to a complete stand still at that very moment and I had become the center of attention.

They all waited with a deep stare of despair, I could just feel it from each and every one of them that stood in that kitchen that day. I hear a voice, coming from outside as a figure entered into the kitchen saying, "Well, anyone hurt?" It was my father, it seems that time went by at a very slow rate; however, it was only minutes, as he ran around the fence to catch up to where I ran into this townhome. I looked at him for just that moment, that stinking moment, where I totally forgot these people were waiting for an answer, keeping their eyes traced onto me for some sign of relief. I shook my head no, meaning there wasn't anyone hurt, but that's all it took. All hell broke loose; everyone was crying and screaming, falling to the floor, people running out of the townhome, it was just a bad scene altogether. I was just answering my father as to his question; if anyone was hurt, but they took it another way in the meaning, was the man in that bathroom alive!

Well, regardless of my answer, the poor gentleman died of a massive coronary, a tear in his heart as I found out through the coroner a few days later. I attended this man's funeral and come to find out; he was the father of my sister's good friend. What a small world, what a very small world indeed.

Psychic Profiler The Real Deal

At this point in my life, wanting to become a law enforcement officer, I knew God had other plans for me. After all those years of anticipating my future, delving into every testing opportunity possible with many different police agencies, I came to a conclusion that wouldn't sit well with many people. I thought long and hard on my next decision, which would take my life down a road in a complete different path. I called up the precinct where I was just hired on as a Police Officer and broke the news of my intentions.

I didn't want to go into law enforcement any longer, but help out in a different manner, a manner that would prelude everything I come to learn. The individual on the other end who took my call that day, instructed me to contact another person who was to help me in my decision. See, you just don't get hired on and all of the sudden, quit! I ended up speaking to a gentleman, who in turn, was involved in creating a working tool for first responders who quit under duress.

I agreed to have a Captain, Sergeant, and members of a film crew, come to my home for a filming segment of this nature. The funny thing is, I wasn't stressed out, I wasn't unnerved by my chance happening with the man in the washroom, no, I just felt very deep within me, I had another purpose now and a different direction I would be taking. The set up began, as they brought in cameras, lights, and clipboards to write on. The questioning began in the manner of, who I was, was my intentions proper in wanting to become a police officer etc. Then, came the big question! "Why did I decide to call it quits when I just got hired?" They were looking for an emotional breakdown in my life, something that would be obscure to the normal, but I was an open book, with nothing to hide whatsoever.

Now, imagine you being me, looking at several people who are completely in trance, glaring back at you and waiting for a magical answer. I spoke up, telling them exactly what happened in that washroom, my entire encounter, and the fact, I felt a different journey was at hand for me. You should have seen the look on their faces! Yes, they were waiting for a meltdown from me, tears, anguish, something that would be of a drama-packed, Emmy Award Winning performance, but they got the truth. A subtle, honest explanation that even by the standards of trying to find some type of duress in me, they couldn't.

Their jaws hit the floor and by the looks on their faces, they seemed more inclined to be spooked, more so than me. The interview was over, the fastest twenty minutes for nearly an hour of set up time, looking for tears and an unwavering, crumbling man, who couldn't possibly take being in the line of fire, I guess. The Captain walked over to me, shook my hand and explained that the filming they were doing was a working tool for many forces to get a better understanding of police, firefighters, EMT's who quit their life's work because of stress. He made mention that I seemed like a really down to earth person, with no such attributes whatsoever, however, they would still like to use the filming of me in their movie. Well, wouldn't you know it! I became a movie star after all at age twenty-one! Not what I was really hoping for, nor did I really want to be seen as something or someone who just didn't have it together. Nevertheless, I'm in that training film, a tool to exercise further education for our first responders and those who want to seek a profession in this field of work. I'd be the calmest interviewee on film, I'm sure of it!

Bills' Miracle!

Friday, November 17th, 2017 at 9:26 PM, I receive a desperate text message from a lady in my hometown, concerning her husband in the ICU Unit at the Hospital in Sarnia, Ontario, Canada. "Robbie I know you are very busy, but I need your advice. Is there anyone in Sarnia who can do a reading on my husband who is in the ICU and unable to communicate. I know he can tell us what the problem is or how he feels."

I sat staring at what I had just received, as I felt helpless in looking for the information to tell Julie and didn't want to worry her at all. See, I was in Virginia, filming a new television series and it was the wrap up of an entire year of production. What could I say or do, I felt entirely dislocated in giving advice being so far away. I responded by saying, "I'm sorry, Julie, for what you're going through. I honestly don't know of anyone credible enough in or around our area in this, what you ask. I'm in Virginia filming this weekend at present. Wish there was someone. Sorry." I continued to glance down at my phone while speaking with my wife on the matter. The production team was setting up for B-Roll footage and we were all on set when the text came in.

I knew for some reason, I had to be in Sarnia to help Julie and her husband Bill, but it would have to wait until this weekend of filming was complete. "I should be back on late Monday night. If you speak to the doctor advising him you want to bring me in, and he agrees, I can come on Tuesday."

I was hoping that they would be ok with this, allowing me to see Bill and help Julie with her request. It's a funny thing with doctors at times as this being an ICU Unit case. It's not normal practice for hospitals or doctors to allow someone to come in and give diagnosis or anything close to that in this regard.

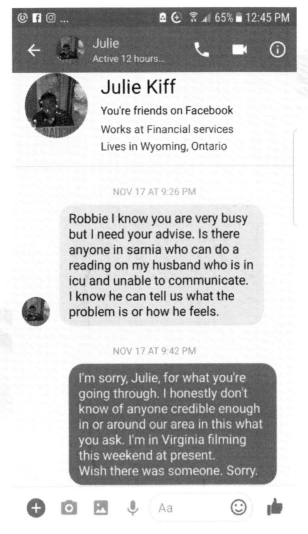

Psychic Profiler The Real Deal

The urgency of this conversation was escalating all the while we were corresponding back and forth. You could feel how important this is and it seemed like the eleventh hour for some reason. Julie continued to text me explaining, "The doctor has no business in it. He's in the ICU and has a team. A native friend saw a medicine man and he has spiritual gifts in his room. They are very good there.

I don't need to ask, they're ok. I would be absolutely beside myself, if I could have you see him on Tuesday. I need someone to get into his mind. I'm so thankful, if you would. I don't care what the fee my husband is worth a billion dollars". I read what she wrote and my heart melted. See, this is what it's about; it's about the love for life. I answered her back, saying I'd be there on Tuesday.

All weekend, the entire time filming, I never once lost sight of Julie or Bill; they were constantly on my mind and in my prayers. My wife and I discussed the situation throughout those days, which kept me focused on my work at hand as well. It seemed that time was going by very slowly, which with anyone who is anxious to do something well by others or good in your day, it seems to go that way at times. Nevertheless, Sunday rolled around with anticipation of a long twelve-hour journey back to Canada from Virginia. Filming had wrapped up nicely as both the Director along with the Producer were pleased at what they had on film , so on the road my wife and I went, headed back home. We pulled into the driveway late at night on Sunday, beat from the long day of travel. I messaged Julie to let her know that I had made it home and would be visiting her the next morning at the ICU.

Julie explained to me over the phone that she had spoken to the Doctor and he was ok with me coming in. She went on to say, "I have to say, he is very sick and has bags for his fluids. He's not awake, very sad looking with all the wires and hoses". My heart fell again, knowing Julie was so worried about how Bill looked for you could tell she just wanted the best for everyone and that moment. She has a GREAT heart!

It's now the morning of, I'm still a bit tired from that long trip and believe me, and I didn't sleep much that night. Over coffee, I tried gathering my thoughts, trying to put perspective on what was about to take place with me going to the hospital. I'll be honest, yes I was a bit shaken to the fact, however, it's not the fight you worry about, its if you don't stand up to do that fight is what bothers me. That is what I kept telling myself while I stared out the window in the kitchen.

On the drive over to the hospital, many things crossed my mind, such as, my own life, family I've lost at times, how much that hurt and still does. I had to do something and the pressure was on, I needed guidance, something Devine for intervention, hopefully the right answers. I pulled into the parking lot, glaring at this huge hospital, shaking in my car. It's not easy dealing with such seriousness of a distress call, however, here I was, a guy from the same hometown as Julie and Bill. I closed my eyes, praying, asking for help in whatever God wanted me to do. I eventually made it up to the ICU Unit and as I rounded the corner, I saw Julie sitting alone in the waiting room, her head turned looking at me, and it was like there was a sense of relief.

Psychic Profiler The Real Deal

We embraced, and then she punched in the code that lets you into the ICU Unit itself. She took me over to where Bill was laying; my eyes immediately enveloped the entire room. A little unnerving to-say-the-least, but I had to stay strong for Julie, holding my emotion in. Walking over to Bill, you could clearly see the distress his body was in. The machines were doing the breathing for him, he was hooked up to several IV's, tubes coming out of his side and who knows where else.

He was in a laborious mode of breathing with his eyes open, pings from all the machines going off around him, monitors with numbers of this and that. It was a frightful sight and I knew we had to do something, something to give answers for the condition he is in. I took off my hat, clasped my hands together, closing my eyes and prayed to Jesus. I asked for his love for Bill and to guide us in answers for what he was going through. I asked for Jesus to allow Bill to speak to me, to give me some type of indication of anything that I could relay to Julie who was standing right next to me.

I started hearing, "Toxic Neurological, Brain Swelling, Wrong Medicine, Time To Heal, Covering Up!" This is exactly how I heard what I was hearing! After praying for a few minutes, maybe five, I turned to Julie and she immediately looked at me saying, "Oh no, it's not good is it!?" I quickly spoke up saying, "No, everything is fine, this is what I heard". She explained she was going to go over this with the Critical Care Unit Team and get back to me. I received a text from her not long after in the afternoon.

It was a bit disturbing to learn the fact they declared Bill brain dead, wanting to remove him from life-support while offering no hope to Julie. "Hi Robbie update… I asked his doctor who is new today and what is Neurotoxicity? She wanted to know why I asked this! I just said, what is it and how does it happen? She started naming things and then told me drugs as well. She then asked the nurse what drugs is he on? The nurse started telling her and the drug I believe with others that caused this they are still giving him!!!! I lost my shit! I swear the whole ICU heard me.

She then told me, 48 hours I had to make a decision, as Bill has no sign of functioning brain and I would need to make a decision based on what he would want. She basically told me, he was brain dead! I left for an hour to sit in my car and cry. I mustered up what I could to go back. Well, everyone was running around, giving me answers, the neurologist, finally showed after two weeks.

She said, 'no way he is brain dead and calmed my fears and wanted to know what Doctor said this. She is going to do another EEG. She said, due to all the trauma, his brain is just slowed to allow healing. So, no one wanted to do anything until I questioned and went postal. Thank you for your help! It started the whole process of getting more help. You were bang on. Oh, and when you said cover up for errors, 150% right!!!!! I owe you!"

Psychic Profiler The Real Deal

Bill has been in the hospital now, by this point, nearly fifty days, and declared brain dead. Sometimes, science isn't the answer, sometimes, doctors get it wrong, sometimes, well, we all make mistakes in life, but let's look at the good side of this, and how faith, prayer, and someone with ability was able to walk into an ICU Unit, restoring the life in a human being from the answers from God.

Proof is in the pudding as they say, as this is well documented on many levels through being there, text messages, hospital records, Julie, and of course, Bill!

Today, Bill is able to sit up, wide awake, talking, eating, and aware of his surroundings, utilizes his arms, but at present can't walk on his own. This will take time of course, as his brain learns all over, healing from this traumatization of the wrong medication, which was disabling him. Since the good of this has come about, Julie has come on a radio show expressing the truth behind this mess, which occurred and written a bit of an explanation placing it on my website for all to witness. It's a true miracle in the every sense of that word, coming from God, without a doubt. I told Bill one thing while I was there praying for him, he is to give me a handshake when he is much better from this ordeal. Julie wanted to pay me and she did mention whatever it costs, I looked her in the eyes and knew. My payment is that handshake!

God Bless Julie and God Bless Bill!!!

Julie Kiff's Letter

What you have just read in the situation of my husband Bill, every word Robbie speaks in this written chapter, and what happened is the truth. I have known him through the paranormal community for some time. Robbie lives in my hometown, and I have attended events he has organized in the past. I was at my wit's end, seeking help for word that my husband of thirty four years will survive. I didn't know what was going on as the doctors wrote him off because he was left basically dead. Of course, I love him so and would not take their direction as I just felt something different. There is more to just medical science and I was searching for the truth, it had to be out there as I wouldn't settle for their explanations.

That's when Robbie came into the picture. I reached out to him and in no time we had set up a meeting. I met him in the waiting room of the intensive care unit at the hospital. He gave me the biggest hug and I immediately felt some relief. We went to see Bill, who I told Robbie looks bad and you could see Robbie was visually shaken. The next while, I really do not remember more than Robbie, praying, and connecting to Bill. I asked him in tears is it bad? He told me, "No, but you must find out, something is wrong.

Psychic Profiler The Real Deal

It has something to do with toxic neurological, wrong drugs, brain swelling. He will be fine, but it will be a long road to heal." So, I asked the doctor a question, which I was advised to by Robbie and found that they had started him back on a drug that caused this whole illness in the first place.

Yes, I went crazy! Robbie was the only one who gave me courage and positive energy, to continue Bills battle, versus, pulling his plug as I was ill-advised. I felt something in his embrace and presence, which said, "Do not give up." For that, I am eternally grateful to Robbie.

Fast forward 2.5 months later and Bill is a miracle, laughing in the eyes of his caregivers. He is a survivor and gets stronger each day. Hope to have him home soon. Then my friend Robbie, you will get your handshake. Actually, we will go for a nice dinner!

Love you and forever thankful!
Julie and Bill Kiff
Sarnia, Ontario, Canada

A Beautiful Side Note: As of today, January 25, 2018, Bill is now home, ALIVE and resting with his wife Julie!

In Memory
Georgina Ann Kiff
1934-2018

Missing Endangered Elderly Lady

March 31st, 2017 started out like any other normal day for me, with an emergency phone call from Pinellas County, Kenneth City, Florida, Sheriff's Office. Law Enforcement Officer, Andy DeLay, who is no stranger to working with me on cases, had an urgent request for me, to assist in the matter of an endangered missing elderly lady. The Bolo went out roughly around 9:30 am that morning and the urgency in finding this lady was immense. As I picked up the call, it became a video conference between me and Officer DeLay and he gave me some specifics on the lady missing. There wasn't much to go on, however, the feeling to get this done quickly was overcoming me, and it was overwhelming.

Once, we disengaged from our telephone call, Officer DeLay was to send me a case file, containing this ladies photo and that is all I requested from him at this time.

(Bolo: Charlene Missing Endangered)

Psychic Profiler The Real Deal

The case file arrived no later than a couple minutes from our conversation and I immediately sat down in my office, trying to render some type of information that would assist in the finding of Charlene. The pressure was on with minutes ticking away in this intense situation at hand.

We began out text messaging back and forth, as I progressed through the motions of channeling Spirit in the hopes of finding the lady soon. Officer DeLay called again, informing me that they were in heightened alert, looking for this lady, as time was pressing to find her immediately. I kept piecing together what information I had coming into me and playing phone tag with the Andy. He informed me they had everyone pretty much on this roll call, out looking everywhere they could for Charlene.

I started to glean visions of water and a bay area, with a rock shoreline. The bay looked curved in nature and I could also see the way in which vehicles had access to this place. I started that procedure to automatic hand drawings, scribing and writing down whatever feeling I had. It seemed very rushed as too, did the emotions coming from Officer DeLay on this situation we had. I began to call him back giving slight information in which he would relay to the others on the force out looking for this lady.

I explained, "I see her on a bus, traveling to an area exactly like a bay, where one could access it easily. The public view of this location I see is a tourist area in my mind's eye and this is how I see her traveling there". I began to give more insightful information as to her being very visible in this area and all this in the interim was being relayed once more over channels of communication with other Law Enforcement Officers out looking. The time in this entire missing person's case took less than an hour and roughly a couple hours later for the news to break on television and newsprint. She had been found ALIVE, just before 10:30 am that same day.

Andy called me with the exciting news and in his voice the elation that she was found safe was the greatest news of the day!

(Text Messages From Law Enforcement Officer DeLay)

Psychic Profiler The Real Deal

Through the miracle of sight and the gift from God, along with
the very commendable efforts from the Law Enforcement themselves,
we were together, able to save this lady's life and return her home
safely to her family. Sometimes cases as such happen fast in the
urgency of it all, like what you've just read above and sometimes they
take much more time. However, this is one case that has a very happy
ending to it and we are grateful for the safe return of Charlene!

Validation And Message From
Officer Andy DeLay

It was just another bright and sun-shiny day at my small West central Florida police department. Things were going slow, and I was enjoying a un-eventful tour of duty. I soon received a call from one of our Assisted Living Facilities saying that a resident had left and not returned in a timely manner. This was not unusual I thought, as the capable residents routinely walk to the nearby K-Mart or pizza place for a bite to eat before returning to the facility.

When I arrived, it was a different story. My routine search for an overdue resident taking a stroll turned into something more serious. A resident that suffered from dementia and Alzheimer's had somehow slipped out of the facility and has been missing for several hours. I reached out to the local Sheriff and other surrounding agencies for assistance in locating the resident. I was very concerned as there were numerous woods, lakes, busy roadways, and treacherous steep banked creeks nearby.

Suddenly, the Sheriff's helicopter went up and there were now hundreds of law enforcement officers looking for an endangered missing adult. After some time searching for the subject and having a knot in the pit of my stomach, I contacted my friend Robbie Thomas. I've worked with Robbie before and I have seen his gifts work firsthand. Robbie soon told me there were rocks and water around the subject.

Psychic Profiler The Real Deal

A-HA I thought, the person had wondered into nearby Joe's creek and fallen down the steep bank. I directed the searchers to look there, but found nothing. Robbie went on to explain how water and movement were factors. He gave details of her taking a bus to a bay area, which included public access. The search went on.

I put out a missing person bulletin to all agencies in Florida, with a focus on the Tampa Bay Area. Soon I received a message that our subject was located across the bay in Tampa, having just got off a bus from St. Petersburg. WOW! Robbie was spot on! The person had just traveled across the bay on a bridge. The causeway leading to the bridge was lined with large rocks.

Without Robbie's assistance, I would not have widened the search as quickly as I did. The subject is safe and sound now because of a team effort between law enforcement and Robbie Thomas and his wonderful gift.

(Officer Andy DeLay, Kenneth City PD)

Assisting In Bringing Home A Daughter Alive From Human Trafficking

"We all know how difficult it can be raising teenage daughters, so it comes as no surprise to parents that we always just don't get along! Well that day came last winter to me and my daughters' relationship! She left home and I never heard from her, only on occasion just to let me know that she was still alive. I was left behind by my daughter and her daughter that she had when she was just 14. An already troubled teenager that had support from her family didn't realize (nor did I) what she was about to endure in the coming months.

She had a girlfriend that I guess she thought cared more about her then we did. This girlfriend introduced her into a world of prostitution. Now occasionally I would hear from her and meet her at certain places and that gave me a sense of relief that she was still okay. I would receive the odd text of her having black eyes or her cellphone was smashed so she couldn't text me. Now I didn't know what she was involved at this point until I started doing more research into it and taking the clues about bruises and phones being broken. I was given a tip one day about her being on websites for escort services. I saw her picture online and she was only 17. This is a parent's worst nightmare. I felt ashamed, totally lost, and helpless! Then came the time where I hadn't heard from her in two weeks.

Psychic Profiler The Real Deal

I was at a total loss as to what to do, I contacted Robbie Thomas through Facebook. I have known Robbie since the 1990's when he hosted an MSN chat room.

He has given me very accurate readings where he has even given me names of loved ones, so I trusted his talent to help me with my daughter. Out of the goodness of his heart, he was able to verify my worst nightmare and supported me through this terrible ordeal of my life. He helped me bring my daughter home ALIVE! He is a wonderful human being filled with compassion and kindness. I hope that my story will help parents, teenagers anybody that might find themselves in the situation I was in! There is hope out there! This is one story where we were not investigating a murder and the ending was truly happy!"

Thank You, Robbie!
Kim Landry-Flewelling
Kitchener, Ontario, Canada

We see this too often on television, hear about it on the news, read about it in newspapers, yet, most families don't realize this goes on in their very own backyard! Yes, and what I'm talking about is human trafficking. Just the sound of those words makes one sick within, and the anger starts to build, knowing the fact indeed it does happen in every city, every province in Canada, or State in America, and reaches far into international borders. What most of the public doesn't understand is, they're out there, and at one time or another, they have had their eye on someone's daughter or son, believe me, this is true!

In Kim's case, a nightmare in the worst was occurring and she didn't want to have anything of it. She immediately contacted my office on a Thursday morning, explaining to me the events that had transpired with her daughter, becoming trapped in the human trafficking, and wanted it resolved before it went beyond anyone's control. She explained, during our first telephone conversation that the detective on the case was at odds as he had nothing to go on, or didn't know what to do next as there were no leads whatsoever.

She was frantic; crying all while trying to explain to me what was taking place in the last couple days leading up to her contacting me for help. Somehow her daughter got caught up in the glamour of the prostitution arena, as a friend of hers was seemingly involved in this, which Kim felt her daughter was enticed and trapped. We discussed many facts and what could have led to this happening and at how much at a loss she was. She needed help in the worst way, mentioning that never in the many years of her knowing and following my work, did she think she'd ever have to call upon me for this type of incident.

Psychic Profiler The Real Deal

I suggested putting on her Facebook posting a statement in regards to her daughters' disappearance because I strongly felt, not only her daughter, but those who were responsible for her daughter's absence, would catch this, knowing we were looking for her and wanting her release immediately. Kim without hesitation made it clear, her family is very conservative, and in no way, shape or form, would she consider posting such a statement because it would be an embarrassment to her and her family.

She implored me to come up with another idea, or some kind of remedy that wouldn't be so controversial. This was the only absolute I had coming to me in my feelings, and when that does happen like this, Spirit is leading the way as I'm just a messenger for the fix. However, this course of action wasn't being greeted in a positive way by Kim, and we ended up finishing our first conversation by phone, with a no go. I left that conversation a bit bewildered and beside myself for the most part because in knowing the fact, she has known of me for so long and that of my work, which just didn't make any sense to me at all for the outcome of our phone call.

The next day being Friday, we again had another phone conversation and you could tell Kim was at her wit's end. A mother who was desperate for her child, no matter what, she wanted her home safely. We took up right where we left off that Thursday night, and again, she reiterated to me the stance her family would take on something so forthcoming on social media. I totally understood her plight, and request on everything we spoke of, however it was coming very evident there weren't many choices to be had for this situation, especially when the detective himself was out of ideas. We needed to find a solution to this circumstance before things got too out of hand, or we would be faced with something more serious, and this wasn't part of the equation. She asked me what she should do, or write up on her social media. I explained to keep it simple and poignant, straight to the point, with sternness, so that those who were watching, would get the picture, understanding to let her daughter go, or her daughter herself to get away from those who were enticing for the wrong reasons.

Kim, being very reluctant, agreed, and within an hour she had posted a very prominent statement in regards to her daughter's disappearance. She called me again, just after posting this statement, feeling very strong about it, in fact, she was pleasantly becoming very strong within herself, and I think that in itself was the turning point for Kim and her daughter. It came down to not worrying what other family members thought or friends, it came down to the urgency of Kim, wanting her daughter home, and nothing was going to stop her from doing so.

Psychic Profiler The Real Deal

A couple days went by, I received a phone call from an elated mother, a mother who so desperately needed an ear to listen, someone who would reach out to lend that helping hand, and I'm so glad she listened to her heart, and I'm happy Spirit listened to her plea. Her daughter was home, and "ALIVE", as she puts it in her letter at the beginning of this chapter. The warm feeling, knowing, the elation Kim had, the sense of her stepping up, taking the lead on focusing on her daughter, and not so much on what others would think, shows how much strength this lady has. My hat goes off to Kim, I'm very happy in the outcome for her and her family because it is a fresh start, something we now share for the rest of our lives.

God Bless Kim And Her Family!

Jessie Foster

This leads me to yet another story of a beautiful mother wanting to find her daughter who has been missing for some time now. Nothing more sinking in one's soul, than that of a missing child and knowing you are helpless in wanting to just reach out and find them. Your heart goes out to all families of missing children, or family members; because you wish there were some magical wand to fix it all.

I had the opportunity to speak with Jessie Foster's mom, Glendene Grant, and let me tell you, what a strong, beautiful woman she is. Jessie has been missing now since March 29, 2006, her case has been featured on many prominent television shows and programs. Glendene is a lovely lady, whose world has been turned upside down because of sick individuals who search out the innocence of children or people to steal away their lives. She is the founder of M.A.T.H., (Mother's Against Trafficking Humans), she advocates for those who are in need of direction and helps in their fight of losing a child to Human Trafficking and is an inspiration as she fights against many of these sick, evil people out there.

I'm too acquainted with the anguish from parents, who have lost their children to this dreadful disease called human trafficking. I've been lucky enough to help two families successfully get their children back from "captors", who thought they could outsmart the police or anyone helping in finding them.

Psychic Profiler The Real Deal

These "animals", these scums of the earth, prey on the innocence, promising them grandeur beyond what is believable, feeding off their fears, their desires and that's when they pounce. Glendene contacted me in reference to her daughter Jessie and I read her, giving her certain details on an individual and more. The details matched in what she already knew and most of it wasn't public information, so I knew we were on to something. One thing that kept coming up to me was the term, "The Shaft!" I'd visualize a long dark shaft, like a mining shaft or entrance of something as such. Glendene then informed me that Jessie went to Las Vegas and again, I sunk in my heart because Las Vegas is in the desert and that desert is vast with mines.

The shovels I saw and working tools, the dirt of it all and pickup truck. There was more in what was said and given to Glendene, which won't be written about, but the hardest part was telling her this as I envisioned it. The tunnel vision, in which I was given this information, comes out like that without hesitation or consideration of whom I'm speaking with until after the fact. We discussed everything, every possibility, and even me being wrong. This is where I truly wish I was wrong and I even pray I am. I want to be wrong on so many levels that I wish everything would not have happened to Glendene and we never knew each other. I want the best for her and her family as my heart breaks for them. There is a hollow in her heart and a piece of her soul taken away, stolen right from her life. Jessie was and is her baby girl, her daughter that these people who took her, really don't deserve to be breathing the same air or walk the same ground as Glendene. God Bless Glendene and her family, my friend always.

Letter From Jessie's Mom, Glendene

Jessica Edith Louise Foster .... Missing Jessie Foster!
My 2nd of 4 daughters.

Jessie went missing on March 29, 2006, which makes twelve years coming up as I write this. Since Jessie's disappearance, her 2 younger sisters have become mothers, making me a grandma for the 1st time, and Jessie an auntie again. Jessie was always a popular girl in school. Right from elementary to high school and beyond.

When she was younger, Jessie always wanted to be in dance classes, go to bible camp, spending time with her friends, anything to keep busy and have fun. As Jessie got older, she was always happy to be with her family. Jessie's favorite holiday was always Christmas, and it was not just her favorite holiday, it was her favorite day of the year.

Sadly, Christmas Day of 2005 was the last day that I or any of her family or friends in Canada ever saw her. She boarded a plane for Las Vegas at 2pm, and never saw her again. Jessie continued to keep in touch with us on a daily basis. March 28th, 2006 was the last time anyone heard from her. She talked to her older sister on the phone several times that day, as they planned her sister's upcoming weekend trip to Las Vegas and Jessie's return with her to attend their step-sister's wedding reception. When Jessie did not return calls to her sisters or myself for 2 or 3 days, we knew something was wrong, drastically wrong. We were all so worried and after 4 days, I called to report her missing.

Psychic Profiler The Real Deal

After getting the run around by not just Jessie's "so-called" fiancé, but also by the police, we were beside ourselves with worry. The police insisted that Jessie was probably in Mexico with her dad and step-family – but we knew better. She would have told us if she was going to go somewhere like that.

After her family came back to Canada, we reported her missing – however, now the issue with the police was that she was probably off starting a new life somewhere and did not want her family to know where she was! It was so ridiculous! After years of Jessie being a missing person, there has been very little done in the investigation, other than by her family. I am not just Jessie's mom; I am her lead investigator on her case. I have not just initiated tips and information to pass on to the police, many of which were never even investigated; I have also got Jessie's case media attention all over the world.

I also founded M.A.T.H. (Mothers Against Trafficking Humans) on April 18th, 2010 and through M.A.T.H. I have educated people everywhere on the crime of human trafficking. I also talk to and help when I can, the families of the missing and murdered.

I have also worked with people like Robbie Thomas, who, thankfully, gives his time and expertise to the families of the missing in hopes to bring answers to what happened.

I am so grateful that 2 years ago when we were approaching the 10-year-mark of Jessie's disappearance, I was in need of help in any way, so I reached out to Robbie Thomas to see if he would be able to give me a reading regarding my missing daughter, Jessie Foster.

He was more than willing to help me. He never asked me for money or insisted that I pay him anything for his help. Even though I have always felt that Jessie is still alive, and Robbie did not think she was. To me, it was a sense of "at least he is telling me something", unlike many others I have turned to in the past.

Since first contacting Robbie, we have stayed in touch and even become friends. I am so grateful for the support I get from Robbie, he is there for me when I need him, and I know he is there for so many others, too.

Thank you, Robbie Thomas, for all you do for so many of us who do not know where to turn.

Glendene Grant

CEO & Founder M.A.T.H.

Mothers Against Trafficking Humans

British Columbia, Canada

Chained In The Basement
Bizarre Turn Of Events

Another case I've assisted in, the family wants to remain anonymous because of the circumstances and backgrounds of many characters that are involved from their family; however, I am allowed to speak of this story, so others can see that there is hope out there, but to get involved in your child's friends, affairs, and know what goes on daily with them.

I was asked to be a keynote speaker at a charity event in Hamilton, Ontario, which was run by a group of ghost hunters from that area. I thought about it for a bit, as I've always wanted to go to this location, aside from Michael Lamport, from Lamport Sheppard being there, it seemed a good thing to do. So, I agreed to go taking part in this event. Everything and everyone who were participating were very nice, and the organizer, along with her husband, seemed ok for the most part, however, there was something strange about them in the feelings I was getting. Shrugging it off, I began to enjoy the night.

I chewed the thoughts with Michael Lamport, of possibly working together in the future and he handed me his card, saying, if I had anything at all in the pipeline to give him a call. The evening was going very well at this point, so I rolled with it, letting things happen as they did. After the event, I returned home and I receive a telephone call from the husband of the lady who organized this event.

He explained some pretty weird things about his wife, which took me back a bit, and thought it best I return to the Brampton area to meet up with him. I reluctantly agreed as I knew this was something police need to be involved with immediately, but he suggested we hold off until he explained the entire situation to me. Sometimes I really kick myself in the ass, being suckered into these long dragged out, totally wrong situations, which evidently only end up getting worse by the minute. However, I must have sucker written all over my forehead, as I did indeed go all the way back down to Brampton to hear this entire freaky story.

I met Dan at a coffee shop, just minutes from coming off the highway as it all seemed to be a totally out of the normal, and a situation I really didn't want to be in. I looked out the windshield of my vehicle, noticing Dan sitting at a table inside this coffee shop. I took a deep breath and proceeded into a story that was about to change the next part of my life forever.

Dan started explaining things, which blew me away about his wife, attacking him the night after the event, doing damage to his van because they were broke and didn't have rent money. He went on to say she insisted on keeping the money from the event and not handing over any of the proceeds generated from it. This didn't sit well with me and Dan started to look more like a criminal in my sight. Out of nowhere, he looks around and states, "My wife is AWOL from the American Army!" I was speechless, just staring at him, wondering what and the fuck did I just get myself into!?

Psychic Profiler The Real Deal

He began speaking about this elaborate story of a young girl, held captive against her will, in the basement of their home they lived in. He went on to describe chains and how Carey would abuse this girl, brainwashing her into thinking, her family didn't want her anymore. I was lost for words, just glaring into everything this guy was spewing at me without hesitation. He was visibly shaking, telling his side of things, all while, looking over his shoulder, as if, someone was watching him or coming for him. My mind was spinning, thinking, "You sick fucker. I just want to reach across this table and break your neck!" He went on, explaining how Carey obtained this girl by enticing her to party with her. The mention of booze and other things crossed his lips, but I was still heated from just knowing and I think in the normal sense of things, much of what he was saying, just went over my head as I couldn't take my eyes off the thoughts of breaking his neck.

He pleaded his case, convincing himself as it seems, of the wrongful way that Carey was solely attributed in doing. By this time, this young girl had been missing for nearly a week, without communication with her family and I just happened to be in the right place at the right time; because, I could only imagine what would have happened to this girl, if this guy didn't crack and confess. I was totally beside myself, telling Dan I had to leave and he had better do something immediately, meaning to do the right thing turning his wife into the police. He seemed very nervous in my last words I spoke, suggesting he was actually going back to let the girl go, regardless of what Carey thought, as he wanted nothing to do with this.

He also mentioned he was finished with her and was calling the United States Armed Forces to report of her whereabouts. At this point, I really didn't give a shit about his story anymore, as I leaned over the table, looking him in the eyes, telling him he better do something now! I drove home with flashes of our conversation going through my mind. The fact, he told me Carey kept this girl chained in the basement because she was going to be bringing extra money into the house, so they could afford their bills!? Oh, that just made me sick to my stomach, so at one point, I had his number on my cell phone from him calling me and I dialed it. As he picked up, I laid into him, telling him, if he didn't let that girl go and call me once he did, I was calling the police once I get home. He reiterated, assuring me he was doing that exact thing, letting her go and contacting the American Armed Forces, as soon as he got back to the house.

Now, here's a twist in this case! I was actually working another mysterious murder case, of a young girl who was found hanging in a park, no farther than two hundred feet from the Police Station in Brampton. I've been on this case for a couple weeks and was heading down to do my Psychic Justice Tour, having this family at my event. The mother of the girl found hung, learned of the difficulties this other family was going through with their daughter missing, putting them in contact with me. Without knowing I have already been going through this with Dan and putting one and one together, things started to look like the twilight zone here. A freaking regular out of the movies fucking sick show and I just happen to be in the middle of it.

Psychic Profiler The Real Deal

I had so much on my mind and definitely too much going on all at once. It was only when I was home, reviewing everything I realized, the girl chained in the basement, was indeed Paula's daughter, who had been missing for a week! Things started to pull together and in recognizing the photo Paula sent me, and the description Dan told me, everything was very uncanny and matched to a 'T'. What are the chances of this being the same girl? What are the chances of that happening, without them knowing, I have just been involved in this situation sitting with Dan? Small world you might say! Oh hell, it really is!

I sat speaking to my wife, sharing everything I've come to learn during my meeting with Dan, and from the look on her face, it said it all! 'Not again!' I remember her words after I told her, "How many freaks are out there like this?" Many things ran through my mind, I mean, I just left there; it was a charity event for a main charitable organization. How crazy can this be, or get? I looked within, trying to find some logical way of thinking how this all was going to play out. It went from a harmless charity event to something totally out of a movie, which was totally bizarre. I called Paula and told her, "I think I know where your daughter is!" You could have heard a pin drop and she spoke in a cracked voice asking me what I mean. I explained, "I just met with a guy who did a charity event I was a presenter in and his description matches your daughters exactly. She's chained in the basement and we need to call the police!" She jumped quickly to telling me, "No, no Police! You handle this please." I was beside myself, thinking, why and the hell would you not call the police?

Paula explained her family is not your leave it to beaver type family and if we could leave the cops out of this she'd appreciate it. I paused, and now it gets even better I thought to myself, but there's this young girl out there that needs help. She again asked me if I would handle this for them and pleaded with me. If things don't get strange in my world, I don't know what does. I reluctantly agree! I became the negotiator to free her daughter, bringing her home in a really peculiar, unrealistic way. Thank God, Paula's daughter is home and unharmed. These are two, of many stories that are of millions out there from loving families who don't deserve this to happen to them. I know this will get read by some of you who care enough to read it, and yes, there will be some who won't, it's those who won't that I wish would. Evil lurks everywhere, and I mean everywhere, from every walk of life, culture, creed, or skin color. It's up to us, as parents, to be vigilant and increasingly more aware of our child's life and include them in the know as well. Keep preaching that sermon, keep pounding it into them because this is the only way reality becomes part of their everyday life.

The last I've heard in conversations with another individual who took part in the charity event organizing, outside of Carey and Dan, was Carey did her time for being AWOL by returning to the United States. As for Dan, there hasn't been any sight or sound from him and no one knows of his whereabouts. It's just one of those Twilight Zone, off the wall, totally bizarre, chance encounters ever. It's something I'll never forget in my lifetime, ever!

Psychic Profiler The Real Deal

I had a couple people comment on my postings that I've read throughout the times, where they have said that they wish they could do what I do or had my job. One in fact, (and I hope she reads this) said, which I thought was the most ridiculous reply ever, but she said, "You have my dream job!" I shake my head at times with people because they just don't get it, they think like those who are looking for the glamour and glitz of it all and get lost in the unicorn effect. This isn't a game or fantasy land, this is for real and for keeps people. I've been endorsed by some of the highest offices in Law Enforcement and Organizations around for one reason. Over twenty-five years of putting my life on hold, to find life for others and give life back to those I could find. There are so many beautiful people out there helping in the fight against crime, who have credentials and experience and for those families living this terrible nightmare, they too have put their lives on hold to bring the message of this disease of human trafficking.

The best advice I have from my standpoint is to give to your children what the other families wish they can give to theirs who are not with them anymore. Love, understanding, and strength in knowing about these perpetrators, who steal and harm human beings, educate your family, keep doing it as much as you can because those that lurk in the dark, wait patiently, ready to take away what is yours.

God Bless All Of You Who Read This & Your Families!

Psychic Justice Tour

The thoughts of doing a tour in 2010 was very exciting with many ideas of how do we go about organizing this one. On the venue, I wanted to bring it for the families and had the wheels spinning. Something different, something no one has ever seen before on a continuous basis! I looked at my wife saying, I don't think anyone has ever done live readings on murder/missing person's cases, let alone do it on a steady basis, live on stage before public viewing with family and police in attendance. This would set precedence and a new to everyone who wanted to see psychic readings, but readings of Psychic Profiling LIVE, giving clues and coming up with significant assistance for police.

Sitting in my office, we looked at many major centers across Canada, the United States and began the tedious planning that took several months to organize. I obviously wanted to start out in my hometown, opening up on the Imperial Theatre, where previously I showed my movie Dead Whisper and packed the place. Of course, I wasn't about to charge for families to come to the venue, but those in the public who wanted to witness live readings, being done on a murder/missing person's case on stage, there was a charge. We wanted the world to witness more than just general readings, I wanted to delve deep into the rarely tapped in area of ability that not too many are willing to step forward to do, let alone step forward to do it live, night in and night out, on stage in front of a live audience.

Psychic Profiler The Real Deal

Next, I looked through the many requests from families and or police, in order to assist in cases of murder or missing person's that would be productive in reading at least two, possibly three families at a time, during a tour stop. We booked Toronto, a second Canadian tour stop, as there were a couple families in need of help in that area and I was partially already beginning to assist them. Then we looked at States such as Ohio, Michigan, Tennessee, Boston, Minnesota, Kentucky, Indiana, Iowa and more. I began to think of my other tours from the past, knowing how long away I'd be away from my family, which becomes tough at times being away from those you love. My wife and I, have a saying for those I do help, we call them, "Perfect Strangers!" Meaning, they're people you want to give everything you can to help because they're perfect and yes they're strangers you go that extra mile for just for the love of people.

Over the many years, I've been away from my family always helping others, either on my birthday, kids birthdays, anniversaries or holidays and let me say this, I love my wife and family very much, as they are totally understanding of the need of others before themselves. In my life's work and devotion to helping, sometimes it honestly becomes a hard choice to make, but I have never said no, nor turned away anyone ever. You strive to do the best you can in life, by giving back as much as you can, for this, I truly believe is where you gain the most out of life. The map was full of opportunity, as many cities were coming up and venues were easy to book. Now, comes the hard part! Where do I book, without causing hurt to many who have been writing my office for weeks and months, knowing that I had plans for a tour?

It, at one point, did come down to cities written down on little pieces of paper and drawing the names out of a hat. Well, we pulled the first place, Kentucky it was, then Iowa, Ohio and finally Indiana. We kept many of the others on a list of possibilities, however looking at the time frame, the amount of travel and time away, it was adding up pretty quick. After having our locations all picked out, it was time to start booking the events. We managed very well getting great locations for performing live on stage with ample room for people from the public to join the event.

Everything was set! Yes, I'm opening up in my hometown, then off to Toronto and then Indiana, Ohio, Iowa and finally Kentucky! We stepped back from looking at what we logged onto the map, seeing how viable this really was in accommodating many families in a real tight tour run. The planning went into bookings, advertisements, radio shows, newspaper interviews and flyers being distributed to each and every location's we'd chosen. It was finally coming together and more of a reality than just a dream.

Sarnia, my hometown and what a thrill of being on stage in the Imperial Theatre, reading a missing person's case of a gentleman, which his wife was told that her husband was dead in Mexico. Well, this wasn't sitting well with me whatsoever, as she had contacted me for a reading about her husband and sent me a photo of him. I most definitely wasn't picking up anything that was told her by this other person, who I felt wanted to just charge her for her misery and that really didn't sit well with me!

Psychic Profiler The Real Deal

(Out of respect for those involved and the purposes of the highly sensitivity of this case, I've decided to use aliases for those involved in this story as requested by "Michelle".)

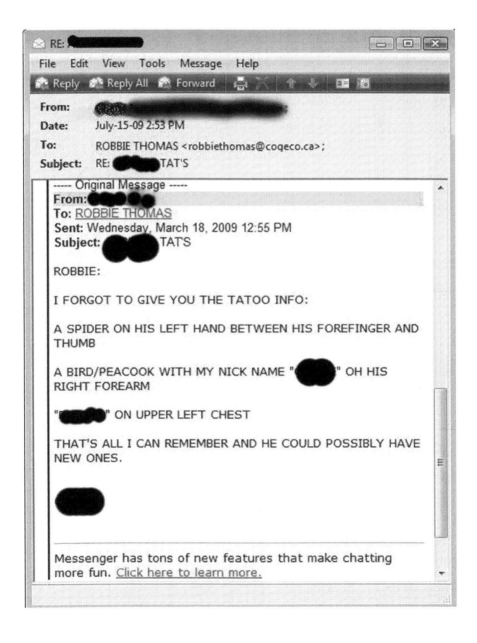

RE:

File   Edit   View   Tools   Message   Help

Reply   Reply All   Forward

From:
Date: July-15-09 2:53 PM
To: ROBBIE THOMAS <robbiethomas@cogeco.ca>;
Subject: RE: TAT'S

----- Original Message -----
From:
To: ROBBIE THOMAS
Sent: Wednesday, March 18, 2009 12:55 PM
Subject: TATS

ROBBIE:

I FORGOT TO GIVE YOU THE TATOO INFO:

A SPIDER ON HIS LEFT HAND BETWEEN HIS FOREFINGER AND THUMB

A BIRD/PEACOOK WITH MY NICK NAME "   " OH HIS RIGHT FOREARM

"   " ON UPPER LEFT CHEST

THAT'S ALL I CAN REMEMBER AND HE COULD POSSIBLY HAVE NEW ONES.

Messenger has tons of new features that make chatting more fun. Click here to learn more.

Michelle contacted me, regarding her estranged husband, who up and walked out of her life back in 1996. It wasn't the fact he walked out on her, rather the way he left that's a bit disturbing. She relayed to me, he left her with two broken arms, in casts, and in each hand, he had duffle bags. One was containing money, the other containing cocaine, certainly not your average breakup by any means. See, Jason was involved as you suspect, in something a little sinister to-say-the-least. Nevertheless, I wasn't there to judge, neither her, nor him, but was there for Michelle to help her in unanswered questions.

Before the show at the Imperial Theatre began, I felt she should inquire about him being out West in Canada, as this was part of a reading I gave her and I felt strongly he was still alive. I gave her the name of the area in British Columbia and I gleaned an impression of him working on motors for boats and something to do with cement. Nothing what I was saying really took a liking to Michelle in the beginning, as it didn't quite make sense because she was already told by an individual who was supposedly a "Psychic" he was dead in Mexico. See, what she was told, was something I don't think anyone in their right mind would say to someone, who is desperately looking for answers of a loved one, however, the damage was done. He was apparently killed in Mexico, in a jail, far in the desert, buried there, along a fence line and to not bother looking for him because she would never find him out in the desert. Interesting you say? Something out of the next horror movie explanation that just had way too much information, but the lack of proper information, which she couldn't give the details of the part of Mexico or where exactly that jail was!

Psychic Profiler The Real Deal

I didn't hear back from Michelle for some time as the show was coming up in the near timeline. Finally, she got a hold of me and was a bit baffled from what the OPP Officer had said to her through contacting the R.C.M.P. in British Columbia. I told her to hang onto most of the information, as I still had to read her live on stage and I didn't want to ruin the surprise of hearing it fresh for the first time. Showtime, and I was ready, the first of many in a line of a tour that would span from Canada throughout the United States.

As I anticipated, this first live audience show was great and the excitement was building. The theatre was filling up and many came out to see this exciting new show called, Psychic Justice.

As I took to the stage, I gave everyone a complete rundown on much of my work over the years of working with Police and families, as well as all my work within the Paranormal Field. I could tell everyone was truly eating this up, as there's never been anything like this put on in my hometown, live on stage like this before or anywhere for that matter. I once before filled this theatre and showed Dead Whisper, my movie from 2005, but this was different, much different.

After briefing everyone on my ability, it was time to show the goods and bringing out Michelle, as she would be the main focus of the night. There were two chairs on stage, a table, and a candle for effect, you know, for the theatrical effect I guess. Anyways, I started to inform the audience that I gave Michelle some homework, prior to coming on stage and me reading her about her husband. The audience was warming up to the things I was explaining because it would lead to much more developments within the show.

When I turned, asking her to reveal any information whatsoever that she had obtained from law enforcement, she was quite surprised to find out the answer they provided her with. "It was a matter of privacy!" This is what she explained to me and the audience members watching. I asked what that meant, her findings from the police and she reiterated, "They told me, it was a matter of privacy and that they couldn't provide me with any information on where he was." Well, don't that beat all, but it gets better and really fast! From out of the darkness, in the audience, a voice speaks up saying, "That's what they told me too!" Everything as you can imagine started to shift now, out to the voice that echoed in the theatre. The spotlight that was just on me a moment ago, was now, searching for that voice in the audience.

Psychic Profiler The Real Deal

It came to rest upon an elderly lady, on the outside aisle seat, about fifteen rows up. I grabbed the mic from the stage, jumped down to the floor level, scurried up to her side, wanting to know what she meant. I gave her the mic, asking her to repeat herself. She said, "I'm his mother and that's what the R.C.M.P. told me and my daughter a couple weeks ago, before coming here to see you about him. They said "It was a privacy issue, he wanted to be left alone!"

Well, doesn't that beat all, again! Yes, I was right about him not being dead, in Mexico, buried outside a jail, along an old fence line in the desert. His mother was elated to hear that from his estranged wife on stage because she actually didn't know I was reading Michelle that night live before everyone, as their relationship was not anymore since Jason left in 1996.

Now, that is a double confirmation, coming from two separate people, who spoke to two separate R.C.M.P. Investigators in British Columbia. I mentioned the exact area as I said early and that was the Delta area of British Columbia. Jason was working on boat motors and they traced him back, to working for a cement company that did driveways and large concrete jobs. He just wanted to be alone and not be contacted at all.

Sometimes, finding out the truth, knowing in hindsight the type of lifestyle someone left from in the first place is a hard pill to swallow. I mean, he left his very own mother and sister, however, there's a side of this story Michelle let me in on. He wanted to get out, so they wouldn't be traced or harmed, by the people he did wrong to in the way of drugs and laundering money. It takes a very selfish individual, giving up the most important part of your life, for a life on the run; however, for the love of family, he did this. I felt for his mother and family, and to think, after all these years, it only took minutes to do some digging to find out Mexico was totally out of the order!

Onward to Toronto's tour stop and reading two families was very emotional for everyone that attended. Here, there were many individuals from the entertainment business as well. I'll leave this tour stop to the words from one of the most respected producers in the business, who came out that night to see the two families find answers to their loved one's cases. Confirmation and validation, were the words for this evening, as much of only what the families would have known as personal information came through for them in abundance.

Psychic Profiler The Real Deal

"I have worked in the entertainment industry for over 18 years and have also been a longtime fan of the paranormal genre. I have never witnessed first-hand events like what Robbie can do. Not only has he been a solid piece of the puzzle in so many criminal cases, he also has the very real ability to reach out to the other side. Having said, 'You have to be there to believe it', doesn't do enough justice. At one live performance that I had attended, he was able to make contact with loved ones and give information that would blow your mind. It really was jaw dropping and you can easily see how he is able to connect and help solve cases. Robbie truly is the real deal!" -Louie La Vella-President/Exec Producer La Vella Entertainment Group Producer/Host - BPM: TV Canada

Ohio was my next stop on this leg of the tour, helping a family with their son who was brutally murdered. Robert was loved by so many and I felt it as I met the most wonderful people in the world during my read for the family. The outpouring of affection for him, his family, and friend was large. I met with them all as they all filled the meeting room we had to rent at a hotel for the show. The number of people the filled this room was amazing! It literally became standing room only.

Before we began this show, I met with Roger Saunders who was helping out in the case with the US Marshal Fire Bomb Expert. Roger and I had a very serious conversation, regarding many aspects on the case, in which I wrote down several of them on a piece of paper, handing it to him, asking him to hold onto them until I needed them the next day. He was puzzled at my request, however, I explained, this is going to show everyone there this is real that the US Marshal and I haven't spoken on the case about this evidence as of yet. He liked that idea and we finished our meeting.

The next night, which I was explaining beforehand, the event was full, with many people waiting in anticipation. I began by introducing myself, explaining what was about to take place for this family wanting answers to the murder of their loved one. I began to speak, giving the reading and this one individual caught my eye, sitting on the inside aisle, desperately keeping focus on me. I turned to the US Marshal, explaining in depth, something you would or only could imagine that would be in a made for TV Movie! He sat dumbfounded, even the family didn't know, until I blurted everything out.

Psychic Profiler The Real Deal

What caught my eye, and really pissed me off, was that young punk, who was playing the family, who was also friends of the guilty, sitting in a seat halfway down in the room on the inside isle, with his cell phone open and on, but trying to conceal it! I knew he had the guilty on the other end, listening into this meeting and when I reached a certain point, I had enough of letting them know, I knew. I said, "Excuse me! Is that a fucking phone you got open & on in my meeting!?" He immediately turned it off and left the room. Everyone there witnessed this as it took place, leaving no doubt in anyone's mind, that punk was part or now is part of this case. One lady stood up and came over to me, explaining that she recognized him as he left the room, thanking me for calling him out on that. Ok, now we've cleared the air, as the rat was caught, not much I released anyways, but enough to let the guilty know they're being hunted! This is where it gets really good! I started to give information that made a couple gasp and stand up! This is where Investigator Roger Saunders who was helping the US Marshal and got me on this case, reached into his pocket, pulling out that magical piece of paper. I mentioned things like, seeing not one, but two insurance deals on this case, the weapon and where it was, oh and wait! Someone stood up, speaking up loudly! But the US Marshal, himself, was amazed and everyone in the room wanted to talk all at once at all the finding just given.

I looked at Roger and he had this look of bewilderment, noticing how much just got uncovered and it jogged everyone's memory! We were now entering a huge part of this case, but I knew already because remember that piece of paper I gave Roger? It's coming true!

True Crime Cases   Robbie Thomas

One lady rushes over to me, excited to explain about the events that took place that night at Roberts's ex-wife's house. Apparently, what I just explained, about the weapon being hidden between walls, jogged memories of that night where Roberts estranged wife, instead of going to the crime scene, had individuals come over to her house in the late night hours to tear out walls and replace them! Interesting isn't it?

Well, I think you get the gist of this and where it is going on every angle that's for sure. I'll leave this case with the words from Roger, the man behind it all and who was very instrumental in the truth being seen.

Investigator Roger Saunders Letter

"I first met Robbie Thomas the summer of 2009, at the paranormal convention in Louisville, KY. Robbie had come into town for the convention and he and some others had agreed to do an interview on wild life radio at the Den Of Sin, which I was a part of. Little did I know the path I was about to embark on with Robbie!

We all hung out after the interview for a bit talking and that's when I got witness accounts of Robbie's talents, not to mention witness them myself first hand. I was curious about some personal things in my life and Robbie touched on them for me. Let's just say, I was more than shocked! Anyways, after the convention, we all exchanged numbers, said our goodbyes, and went on our way.

Psychic Profiler The Real Deal

Fast forward to Psychic Justice Tour in 2010. Robbie and I had been staying in touch through social media and texts. It was typical hey what's up, how's things, until one day Robbie reached out to me, telling me about his Psychic Justice Tour.

Robbie wanted to know, if I knew of any cases here in Ohio that where unsolved that cops/detectives, may need help on cause he would like to include Ohio on his tour. I said I would look into it for him. I went to the gym a few days later and ran into a State Marshall/ Arson Investigator who I had spoken with a lot in the gym. When we were talking, it came to me to ask him, if he knew of any cases for Robbie. Jeff responded by saying, "You know, I have this arson/murder case that is just dead in the water and could use a fresh look so why not. Things just don't add up for me on this one!" So, then at that point, I put Jeff and Robbie in touch with each other and they set the date for Robbie to come to Ohio.

I want to state before I go into this story. Robbie had no access to any file on this case what so ever. It was here in Ohio, under lock and key, until the day Robbie profiled the case. With the family there, Robbie proceeded to Profile the case. Robbie went into great details about the case that no one knew.

He knew the layout of the home, where Robert was first attacked, and he knew how the fire started, the nature of Roberts's injuries. Robbie asked the family about Roberts's wife, and mentioned that he felt she had a hand in Roberts's murder. At that point, the room got quiet, and then they responded by saying, "Yes we have always suspected her in this!" Robbie then said, she has played a role in it, but did not do it herself.

He stated that he felt she went somewhere and waited to hear that it was done. And that that person that did this was close to her. Robbie also gave details of the weapon and where he felt it would be found. All of this info Robbie was giving the family was not in the file. Fast forward again to present day, February 2016. Robbie reaches out to me, wondering, if the State Marshall, would be interested in being involved in this new project he was pitching. I said, if I see him I will ask. A few weeks later, I seen Jeff at the gym and asked, if he would be interested. I kept working out and then I remembered about the case Robbie did, so I asked Jeff, if it had ever been solved. Jeff says, "Huh funny you ask! I have since retired from doing any of that, but just recently got a phone call asking, if I would be willing to interview a guy in prison. He said he has info on this case and will only talk to me".

Jeff proceeded to tell me that this guy started out by saying he didn't want any compensation of time served or anything for this info, he just wanted help getting off of drugs, he did not want to be on them anymore.

Then he proceeded to tell Jeff about this guy he is friends with and spent a lot of time hanging out on his porch, drinking and talking. He said this guy told him about this individual he killed and then set fire to the house and got away with it. Said that he was seeing a girl at the time that was married to this guy he murdered. Said the guy's name was Robert and that his wife dropped him off, and then waited a few blocks away for him while he did it. Said that when he was done he went down, got in the car and they drove off.

Psychic Profiler The Real Deal

Jeff asked the guy, if he would wear a wire and, if he felt he could get the guy to discuss it again. The guy said, "He's one of my good friends and trusts me and will talk about anything with me, He's bragged about it several times".

I could not believe what I was hearing! This guy just told Jeff exactly what Robbie had told the family, 7 years ago. Are you ready for the kicker!? The jaw dropper? When Robbie reached out to me, asking about Jeff and, if Jeff would like to work with him, it was for a show Robbie was pitching to have law enforcement with him as they make arrests on cases he has profiled. And that he felt the case he sat in on here in Ohio was going to have a big break in it real soon and will be solved real soon.

Then less than a month later, after speaking to Robbie, I spoke to Jeff Broughton and found out that Robbie was indeed correct yet again.

Robbie Thomas is 'THE REAL DEAL'. I have witnessed it in person myself. Anyone who denies it, just doesn't know Robbie at all and is a skeptic."

Caesar Ivan Aguilar Cano Case

June 30th 2007, a day I'll remember always, as it has become etched in the back of my mind forever. With Canada Day being July 1st, my family, friends and I, were all gathered in the backyard, celebrating the holiday with much food and fun. It was your typical hot summer day, with nothing to worry about and the grill was cooking all our favorite treats. This is the time of year being on a border town from the United States, we get the luxury to celebrate all week long, as the American holiday falls on the 4th of July. As the festivities were just warming up, a phone came into my office, where my wife answered, summoning me quickly into our home. I could see in her facial expression that there was nothing good about this call.

She explained to me, it was a call from Kentucky and that it was of urgent concern. I entered my office, picking up the telephone only to discover the frantic voice of lady named Francis, who at the time, had difficulty getting the words out fast enough, explaining a young four year old boy had gone missing in Louisville. She explained, there was a four year old that had gone missing and the police were out searching for the him. She made mention she contacted, Detective James Bland, from the Louisville Police, explaining to him who I was and how I could be of assistance in this child's disappearance. We discussed the urgency of the matter as well as what little details they had to go on at the time.

Psychic Profiler The Real Deal

It seemed very much a bleak situation, as I could sense the frustration being expressed over the phone from Frances. She forwarded onto me, via email, a photograph of the little boy, his name and that's all I had to go on in hopes that channeling spirit of his whereabouts would be fruitful. I literally gasped, glancing at his photo, feeling the emptiness deep within myself, almost like a rock hitting the bottom of a deep well as my stomach sunk. My thoughts eluded me as I became numb to the point all I could do is stare at this beautiful little four year old little angel. I snapped back from my thoughts to what was going on prior to this phone call and the people who were in my backyard celebrating Canada Day. I was torn between this poor little boy gone missing, but surely they'll find him, everything would be just fine, I thought to myself while still looking at his photo.

I reluctantly spoke up, saying I couldn't assist at this time because of prior engagements and the fact we've planned this celebration party for weeks now. I had company from out of town, across town and I had mixed feelings rushing through me, as I knew there was something more than that of my selfish thoughts. As I hung up from speaking with Frances and explaining I had prior arrangements, I turned to only see the look on my wife's face all while hearing those words that will ring with me always.

She looked at me, demanding me to call Frances back to help in any way I could. She was right, there was nothing proper in me saying no and for what, a party, where a child's life was in the balance. I have no idea what came over me at that time to say no, but I know from that moment on, after my wife telling me to call Frances back, it was the right thing to do.

After calling back, I sat with paper on desk and pen in hand. I knew what I had to do and began a long tedious channeling of many Spirits, calling upon them to assist in this quest for answers. Nothing ever comes easy, especially when it's dealing with missing children or murder cases at any time. Your entire being becomes an instrument of dialogue, a sophisticated tool of guidance from a guiding hand of those on the other side, who are there, watching and speaking, very loudly, within the mind's eye. I started the session, becoming very in tune with everything around me and within me. The moment of complete silence rendered a deafening, loud interlude, which started to produce pictures and sights of many things I wasn't familiar with. It became much in the way of intervention, as my pen to paper illustrated in the automatic hand drawing taking place in my office.

I had to slow things down, so I could grasp something, anything that was being shown me because it had a steady pace and I was trying to make heads or tails out of what was being shown to me. Things were happening readily, which at every time I put my pen to paper to draw or write what I was seeing; I was whisked off to another scene of something completely different. At this point, I had to ask questions, interjecting to try and take some type of control on what was coming in from Spirit. I asked for landmarks, something that would be recognizable by those who lived in that area or for the police to say we have a good hit.

Psychic Profiler The Real Deal

I sat in second person, asking these questions and directing that interview, if you will, as if, I was conducting what should be coming into me. This is as sound mind an explanation I can give, as to how the proceedings took place during the session of many voices coming through because the interlude was having its moments.

Yes, I had uncertainty, much in the way of everything being thrown at me all at once, left and right, this, and that. It became an unsettling observation of many flashing photos, viral voices, directions; it started to intimidate me at certain points. I felt the post, during and prior, to everything that was happening to this beautiful little boy and in the same sense, I had to keep my wit's about me, searching for that one clue that was certain.

It felt, like I was being sucked into a very deep unknown, yet I knew what I was here for and my ability to do this kept me in stride with was presented me. As strange that sounds, sometimes you really have no control over or what information they want to reveal or what you ascertain from connections as such, it kept me idle in focus and wanting to proceed. I just kept faith, pushing forward, forward to find the answers that were so desperately needed in searching for Caesar, for this beautiful little boy.

Suddenly, I'm given four dark circles and shown stadium lights! My pen scribbles rapidly what I was witnessing, placing those four stadium lights down onto the paper in front of me. This took me back, but again, my pen continues to draw steadily while many images were crossing my mind's eye.

I began to ask questions, such as, "Give me an area closer to where you are? Show me something that is happening right now, where you are?" The images of men, in orange vests and construction taking place on the road area, which I felt was very close to where Caesar might be was flashed in several ways.

It kept coming through many different angles, almost like I was hovering around that area, in order to get a clearer, focused view, on his whereabouts. The sights and sounds seem to blend together at times, but I kept pushing for more, there has to be more, come on, give it to me now, I thought. The anxiety was tremendous in the extreme that I was anticipating a monumental moment soon to come, you could just feel it.

**Drawing by Robbie Thomas
in respect of Cano case**

Psychic Profiler The Real Deal

So, I scribed down on the paper in front of me, men in orange vests and construction, very close to where he was kept. I went back to the stadium lights and I hear, "Off, stadium lights off!" Once again, I'm finding myself drawing four stadium lights, in representation of four circles and write, "Stadium Lights (underlined), Dark, Like Off, Not Far Away." Now, I know he's not far from all of this, which is being shown me and the excitement of possibly getting some definite answers and hopefully save his life and bring him home.

I get flashes of pictures of two other boys, along with the voice that says, "He's a repeat offender, other boys!" This really didn't sit well with me whatsoever! My attunement started to change with much anger within, knowing what that meant. Only a monster of unfathomable proportions crossed my mind and every deep seeded good part of my being, wanted to reach through the sense I had and break this guy in two. I started to become very ill to my stomach, cramps began up and down my sides because I knew, I was thousands of miles away from this little boy, how on earth can I prevent anything happening to him?

Frustration building, anger building, hate towards this individual, seeding its way into my very thoughts, which was a huge distraction in doing what I had to do, which was to get as much information as possible and as quickly as I could. I didn't want to hinder this situation or channeling whatsoever, so I had to remove myself for a brief moment in order to gather my thoughts and realize the focus at hand.

I knew we were pressed for time, I sensed it with every ounce of my being, however, the human side, and the emotions were getting the best of me. I sat back down to begin once more, trying to configure the best possible evidence for police and those looking for Caesar.

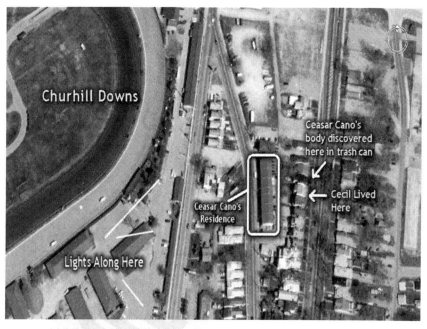

A small room is flashed before me. I see a damn small room! What and the hell's going on? Flashes of stadium lights, vests, construction, men in those vests, little flags in the ground, car sounds and this dark, dank, small room, it kept repeating itself, over and over to me during this session, as my pen put to paper everything I was seeing. The disturbing situation became very dire at this point, there wasn't any time to waste, as everything I was seeing, I felt in my gut, sensed there was something more sinister and evil here.

Psychic Profiler The Real Deal

No time to waste, nothing worst sounding than the clock in the room ticking slowly and it seemed every second that did tick off, sounded louder and louder, making each moment more intense. It became a time within itself, almost like being trapped or held hostage to a source you couldn't touch or see, it just sucked the very life out of me.

Tears started to well up in my eyes, and once again, my emotions took over as the despair of dire need kept pushing my shoulder. "Come on Robbie, Come on for fuck sakes! Calm down and do this right, don't be such an idiot." This is what I was telling myself aloud, as I paced back and forth in my office, staring at the notes and images I've been given that were etched on paper.

Give me more, I need much more, and now, I kept thinking to myself, the abundance of information that was privy to me that Spirit was showing, seemed like an endless sea of slow, rowing, waves that were hesitant to get to the point. The word or name, "John", I hear, writing it on the paper as my vision I'm gleaning is as if, I'm standing on the front porch of the murderer's home and I see a clearing straight ahead, I can see a stadium. Here again, stadium lights like off, as I continue to scribe everything I can onto paper. I know now, he's close to a stadium with a name that has John attached to it, it was a first definitive sign I had of his whereabouts.

I'm quickly getting my feelings mixed in with the ability to stay attuned to this case, it's something that becomes overwhelming, yet, I continue. I struggle to look beyond the repeated information being transcribed onto paper, seeking more, much more of an indication, something substantial to tell the police. A face, yes a face! It begins to come in to view while my pen once again, scribbles shades of this character that seem to mimic who he is. As the information continues to multiply in many directions, I've developed this tunnel vision, which resembles being one sighted and that nothing around me exists any longer, a complete, straight, tunnel vision of information pouring in.

I state loudly while I sit at my desk, "Please, give me a name of a place you are close to. Can you give me a name of a place?" I hear immediately, "Juan!" So, I write, "Juan", on the piece of paper that is now becoming a canvass of many different things that are a puzzle waiting to be pieced together.

Psychic Profiler The Real Deal

I hear dogs barking and it's as if, I look to my left, seeing dogs guided to that dark, dank, room in a basement area. I write dogs/puppies on paper, but the sense in me feels something different. This isn't going as it should, something is terribly wrong here! I feel the static of being withdrawn from this intense encounter that the word being pulled back is less of a term I would use. It was like an immediate black out, nothing before me, nothing! I feel like a door was just shut in my face and I'm being shoved aside with nothing more, feeling at a total loss from everything. I tried desperate, looking within to see, if there was anything at all, something I could grasp and start again, but there was nothing, just a blanket of empty nothingness.

Oh, I'm right mad, no, I'm pissed! "What and the fuck just happened here!" There was a connection; it was very strong, and now, nothing, nothing whatsoever. I stand up from my chair, parade around my office, throwing my pen across the room, thinking it's done, it's over. I can't comprehend what has just taken place, however, I have this sinking feeling once more, and it isn't what I anticipated at all. There was so much coming through, I diagramed, wrote out everything, to only come to a complete stop like that, I wasn't having it, no frigging way. I had to press on, searching deeper with Spirit and I'd sit waiting for ten, to fifteen minutes, before things started to slowly play out once again in short bursts.

I continue now, it's his face and the pen is moving on the paper once more. I interject speaking out loud, "Please give me his name! Just give me his name, so we can help you!" The room is very quiet, until the vibration of a name is heard. I hear clearly "Cecil!" I ask, "Is this the man I'm drawing? Is this his name?" I hear very clearly "Cecil!"

I immediately write his name above the face that I was drawing, putting an arrow directed to his head, knowing now, we have a name. This was the breakthrough I was waiting for, something substantial, so that the Police and those looking for Caesar, could search out this name given and hopefully lead to the rescue of this four year old little boy. I was anxious in getting this information to Frances who was the liaison in Kentucky, as she was sending information back and forth to the lead detective on the case as requested by him.

With all the information that came in and this sheet of paper in front of me filling up, I knew we had many good leads, something the Police would be able to utilize in piecing everything together to profile of who this was. After completing everything I possibly could during this channeling, I forward it onto Frances, who in turn connected with Detective James Bland and sent a copy to the news network in Louisville. My fingers were crossed and my heart was crying out, for I knew, something terrible befell this beautiful little Angel. My anger in the deep seeded knowing as I sensed his life being taken from this monster, made me cringe, however, I had to try and disregard this information through feelings coming through and start the next day for more. As I continued to look over my information and felt nothing more coming into me, I felt I had everything I could have received, forwarding on the information and held out for the better that I was wrong in my sensing.

Psychic Profiler The Real Deal

There were the odd phone calls back and forth in connection to the case with Frances as we sat on pins and needles, waiting for the detective(s) to speak of something from everything that transpired. A couple days later, I get a call explaining they used all my leads and that these were the leads that got mentioned on the news from the Detectives. A few more days passed and our worst imagined nightmare did come true, they had found this little boy's body in the garbage. This monster discarded this angel like a piece of trash and now, the world knew what had happened to Caesar. My heart fell to the floor finding out this news; I just wish I was wrong in my perception of what I was seeing.

(Below are emails sent from my office to Kentucky for the police to have the information on this case. We've blurred out the email addresses of the Police and investigator helping on the case.)

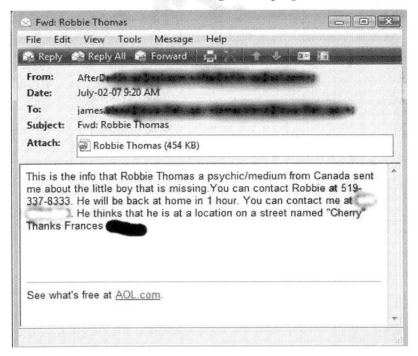

Fwd: Robbie Thomas

File   Edit   View   Tools   Message   Help

Reply   Reply All   Forward

From: AfterD
Date: July-02-07 9:20 AM
To: james
Subject: Fwd: Robbie Thomas
Attach: Robbie Thomas (454 KB)

This is the info that Robbie Thomas a psychic/medium from Canada sent me about the little boy that is missing. You can contact Robbie at 519-337-8333. He will be back at home in 1 hour. You can contact me at ____. He thinks that he is at a location on a street named "Cherry" Thanks Frances

See what's free at AOL.com.

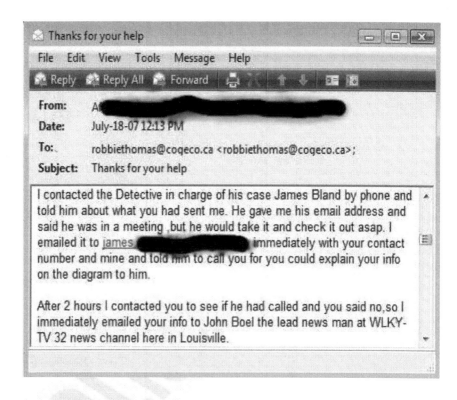

Here is the full extent of the email above (I've copied and pasted it below for understanding of the process and the conversations that took place during this case. The intricate moments from the time I was contacted, until the time of my office responding in assisting in the case, much transpired during and after the arrest of, Cecil Eugene New, for the murder of Caesar Ivan Cano. In the respect to everyone involved in this case that reached out to bring this monster to justice, I've kept all documentation preceding the initial telephone conversation with Francine Etienne for verification on this case.

Psychic Profiler The Real Deal

Dear Robbie,

I want to thank you for all your help when I called and asked you to help find Ivan Caesar Aquilar-Cano on June 30, 2007. He had wandered away from his home and had not returned. The police here had not issued an amber alert because they said there was "no evidence" that he had been abducted.

This is a shame because he had been missing for more than 24 hours and there should have been one put out no matter what. He was only 4 years old. You have always been there to help when called upon and took this case and started communicating with little Caesar.

On July 2nd you emailed me a diagram with a picture of the man who had him and the name, "Cecil", above it with an arrow pointing to the man's picture, you also had 4 round circles that had stadium written under it and that it was not far away from Caesar's home.

You explained to me these were lights like you would see at a stadium, but that they were out. Your description of this man had a lot of details, he picks his nose a lot, or plays with nose a lot, smokes a lot, shoes untied or undone, he was wearing a muscle shirt and gray or white track pants.

You also said Caesar was locked in a small room, that this man had pictures of other small boys. You also had John and Juan written down and the number 1478. I took the John as meaning "Papa John's Cardinal stadium' there are stadium lights there. You wrote down men in safety vest, orange and yellow stripes.

I contacted the Detective in charge of his case James Bland by phone and told him about what you had sent me. He gave me his email address and said he was in a meeting, but he would take it and check it out asap. I emailed it to, james.bland@xxxxxxxxxxx.xxx, immediately with your contact number and mine and told him to call you for you could explain your info on the diagram to him.

After 2 hours I contacted you to see if he had called and you said no, so I immediately emailed your info to John Boel the lead newsman at WLKY-TV 32 news channel here in Louisville. I tried to find the number to contact Christopher 2x our community activist here in Louisville; they were reporting that there was a psychic here in Louisville that was with him and the family working on the case. The next day, I again tried to call Mr. Bland, but just got his voicemail. I tried the same with Mr. Boel.

On Saturday, July 7th they announced that a small boys body had been found by the garbage men as they were getting ready to compact their truck. The whole community knew that this was little Caesar and on Monday, July 9th, the coroner confirmed that this was him. The sad thing about this is that all of your clues were completely right.

Police brought in the cadaver dogs and they followed the scent to a (first clue) man's house right behind where Caesar lived. The home was that of a man named "CECIL"(second clue), His home is in eye view of Papa John's Cardinal Stadium (third clue). The man's middle name is Eugene, in Spanish it is pronounced Juan (4th clue).

Psychic Profiler The Real Deal

Caesar was found right behind where he lived (5th clue). On the day Caesar came up missing the police and searchers went door to door asking people if they had seen him. One of the people they asked was Cecil, he said he had seen him pulling up LG&E utility flags in his yard and he told him to stop and go home(6th clue safety vest of workers who were putting down flags).

Cecil is a convicted child molester who had served time for molesting nine and ten year old boys (7th clue). I also emailed Mr. Bland and John Boel the Ky. sex offenders' online page and told them to look at it.

On Monday I left a message on Mr. Boels voicemail asking him for Mr. 2x's phone number and he called back and left me a voicemail with his number.

I gave you his number and Mr. 2x was really moved with all you had come up with and said those were the best leads the police could of had and he was going to contact the Chief of police and the detective in charge of the case to find out why they never followed your leads. The next day I contacted him and he told me that the police said they had followed "all" your leads they had gotten and they made an announcement that night on the news that they have followed "all" the leads.

This sounds funny to me that they would do this. I felt they were personally trying to cover their butts per say because Mr. 2x is always open with the community and afraid he was going to let this out to the media, if they had acted right away he would be alive today. They waited until he was found dead then followed your clues and went to Cecil's home and gathered evidence. Mr. 2x told me on July 16th that they had told him that they had followed your clues.

Now, Cecil is in hiding saying he is in "fear of his life" because the circuit courts office had released info by mistake that they had a search warrant issued for his home. On the day they found Caesar residents reported seeing Cecil outside in the early hours of the morning, why it was still dark moving around peoples trash cans.

Then he himself disappeared. Why disappear if no one had approached you yet?

Robbie your gift is one that cannot be topped, you came here for the Bardstown fire and then spent time trying to help find little Caesar. I thank you from the bottom of my heart.
May God always bless you in everything you do!

Frances

Psychic Profiler The Real Deal

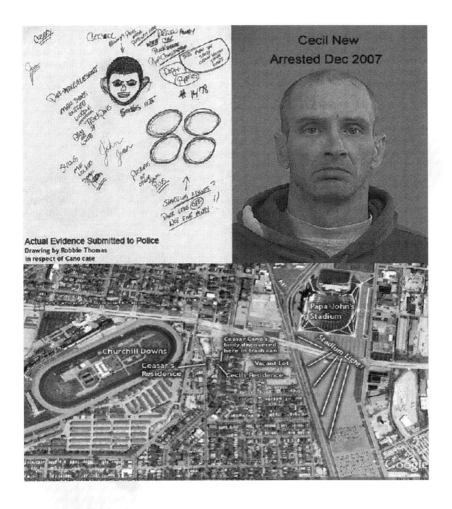

The Comparisons from the drawing on paper from seeing through the eyes of a four year old little boy, which came in flashes quickly, are uncanny as it resembles the murderer Cecil Eugene New. I was given the name of 'Cecil' and it is clearly marked on the paper above with an arrow pointing to the head of the murderer himself.

God Bless, Caesar Ivan Cano and his family. May God Comfort his family and give Caesar peace in Heaven... Amen!

Victoria Stafford
Angel Taken From Us

"My family became acquainted with Robbie Thomas, as we desperately searched for my niece Victoria (Tori) Stafford. Robbie contacted my mother online, offering his services. Never having been in this type of situation before, we were willing to take any offer of assistance to help us locate Tori. Many things that Robbie told us have proven accurate, though it is his being (rather than his gift), for which I will be eternally grateful. Although our situation ended with our greatest fears, I find peace in knowing we did everything we could have done to bring Victoria back to our family. Robbie was an integral part of these efforts. Thanks to his gentle encouragement, we found ourselves providing police with information that we had not previously imagined to be of importance. We were given comfort, strength, and support through Robbie's involvement in our greatest time of need. As a result, I will always be thankful that we were blessed with his benevolence. I wholeheartedly believe in his abilities, and I encourage others to accept his willingness to help.

With much love, respect, and appreciation, I say thank you, Robbie."

Rebecca Stafford (Nichols)

Psychic Profiler The Real Deal

"Well, that at the same time, I mean, you're doing these sketches and thoughts before anything ever comes out. Before they even go and investigate it or even find out some of these details, I remember you off air talking to me about the Tori Stafford case and saying those exact things, before they ever even investigated that part. So, I know you were telling me stuff that eventually came true…I'm kind of a skeptic myself, so I kinda, I believe it, yeah, I believe it!" – George Hays, Program Director, 99.9 Fox Fm, Sarnia, Ontario, Canada. (More of this quote and recorded show can be heard at www.robbiethomas.net)

Sitting in my living room, watching television with my wife on an uneventful evening, there was something different and I couldn't put my finger on it. The night was fine with my family; however, unease enveloped feeling within me, began to fester that left me unsettled for the most part. I tried to disregard the feeling, thinking it as just perhaps I was anxious for something or something to happen. The air became suddenly cool to me and that's when I knew something more than just being anxious was about to occur.

It played out like watching television, perceptions, or premonitions of a little girl, walking into a tree line, near a huge pile of rocks, wagon wheels everywhere and buggies. People in Mennonite clothing riding in those buggies. There was a very ominous feeling about this, more of a warning, which was so realistic in the sense it was about to happen in the very near future.

After witnessing this, I glanced over at my wife who had a strange look on her face, as she was observing my behavior during this encounter interlude I was experiencing. With my voice cracked, I explained to her straight out, "I think there's going to be a little girl go missing, with blond hair, no more than ten years of age. I feel it's going to be real soon! I just saw this right now!" That feeling, yes, I've experienced it more than I would like to admit and it's something one wouldn't like to experience, only to find out it really does come true. Premonitions are like a wake in the timeframe of soul connection, they contain you physically, emotionally and mentally, throughout an encounter that is more of a real life experience, rather that of just presuming.

I began to explain more to my wife and the unnerving feeling was something I'm being called out to help from Spirit, as the inevitable was about to occur. A couple days later, it was on the news from a city not far from mine, about an hour and a half away called Woodstock, Ontario. When the news broke, once again, my wife and I just looked at each other in amazement, knowing, there were higher powers, reaching out to me, giving me notice of a happening that was to occur.

We discussed me contacting the family, as I normally never offer myself to families, or police by volunteering because I never wanted to look like an ambulance chaser, so-to-speak, however, this seemed proper for some reason, it was a slight push to do so. I must admit, I was hesitant just for the reason, people and how they would judge this type of approach. Not only that, but the family, how would they be receptive to a stranger, offering his help in such dire moments.

Psychic Profiler The Real Deal

Many things went through my mind, considering this decision, however, in my heart I knew it was the right thing to do. I said prayers, asking for guidance from God, as I was about to embark on a quest to find answers for a family who had none. I looked deep within myself, asking God for them to just listen and, if they didn't accept my assistance, hopefully what I was about to give them in my sketches would help. I began doing sketches of the entire encounter that was shown to me. I started to draw, the tree line, the huge pile of rocks, the many wagon wheels, a laneway, and so much more information, coming through at a steady pace that kept my pencil to paper, as many flashes of things were coming through for this case very fast. I profiled a man and a woman, what I felt and seen of their characteristics, age difference, as the female was much younger than the male, some other things pertinent to this case that most certainly would lend credence to those who done this.

The female wanted to prove herself to the male of being the mother type or good for him. Because of past experiences with missing person's cases, I thought it best to get the information down on paper, so I don't forget anything, which could be of importance and that way things might go a bit faster as well for the investigating officers. Again frustration, anxiety, being scared for the fact what I was seeing, was enveloping me, making me part of what was taking place. I worked at a furious pace getting things down as my wife sat watching me do automatic handwriting and drawing in this respect. I tried desperately to manage the factors that I could before they began to change or fade out of my mind's eye.

The information was free flowing and abundant, which made it very easy for me to speak it to my wife as I did this just in case I forgot anything pertinent. I was able to speak to a family member by phone, Rebecca and was invited down for the candlelight vigil in Woodstock on April 12th 2009. Here is the first time I was to meet Rebecca, Rodney, Doreen and the family. Rebecca wanted to introduce me to the media, as the Psychic going to help in the case, however, as fate would have it, my daughter needed to have something to eat and being diabetic, she forgot her needles back in Sarnia, so we had to leave the candlelight vigil halfway through that night.

The next day, we arranged to meet at the Tim Horton's parking lot in Woodstock, as soon as you come off the highway. The night before traveling to Woodstock for the candlelight vigil, I managed to fax off the information I had sketched out on paper to Rebecca, so she could inform the Detective on the case of my findings.

There were many emails to follow and in each that crossed my inbox, I sat with heart in hand, looking for those answers to all their questions. Victoria was orchestrating everything, she was pointing me in the direction in which to look, what to say, how to address everything. The problem I had was it was coming in very fast, and like a puzzle, I had to sift through so much to make an understanding of what I was receiving. It may have seemed like a daunting task, but it wasn't as this was something I was being directed to do, I was being led by Victoria to help find her.

This was the first step of many I felt, as this would turn out to be a case that needed everyone on board to find this Angel.

Psychic Profiler The Real Deal

Many questions went through my mind all night long, knowing the answers are all in the sketches and my notes I've made that were sent by fax. I tried to separate the fact from the fiction that often runs through one's mind because you always want the good to be the truth, you want the outcome to be completely different than what you're being shown from spirit. Prior to traveling to Woodstock, Doreen, Victoria's grandmother emailed me some very distinctive questions, which I addressed when I arrived the next day.

Re: Robbie Thomas

File   Edit   View   Tools   Message   Help

Reply   Reply All   Forward

From:	Doreen Graichen <
Date:	April-21-16 11:39 PM
To:	Robbie Thomas <robbie@robbiethomas.net>;
Subject:	Re: Robbie Thomas

We've survived, in awkward fashion, a very complicated and difficult event which has had many 'veins' and degrees of complications ever since. It is what it is.

I remember your assistance to us and also can never forget your drawing and speaking about the wagon wheels and people dressed in 'Mennonite' fashion. It has never been out of my mind and when they found Tori, it made so much sense.

I think of you often and look forward to seeing your book. Much success to you on your project Robbie.

Hoping this finds you and your family well and good and looking forward to an exciting new season. God be with you and bless you my friend.

It's strange how so many secrets and darknesses go unnoticed to us as mere humans. But I do still believe in karma. I refer to some family extensions that are and have always been dark elements.

Thank you for reaching out to us. And agree It really has been years since we've had a chance to chat.

Good evening, my friend and God be with you in your endeavours.

Doreen

(Correspondence Between Doreen, Victoria's Grandmom and I)

This is the turmoil, in which, what I do through engaging with the other side, looking for the truth and answers for families often happens. I just knew, from within my heart that I had to assist this family, as Victoria had already reached out to me from Spirit.

It wasn't long before a gentleman and a lady arrived at the parking lot. I felt that these were the ones I was to meet, so I spoke up, asking if it was them. I met Rebecca that day, who quickly became a great friend and I, in turn, hers. We discussed me following them back to the family home, where I met other family members of Victoria's.

A very somber mood was felt within this home and hit me hard, as I crossed the threshold, looking into the eyes of this beautiful family who wondered who this stranger was. I sensed everyone's feelings, knowing their thoughts, seeing a perfect stranger walking into their lives, who said he could help in finding Victoria, seemed a bit overwhelming at this time, however, it was the beginning to much transpiring. I slowly greeted each loving soul in the home while trying to think of the right thing to say. My heart literally fell to my stomach, as the silence was defining, knowing their souls were drained from this terrible happening. Their eyes showed the tears they've cried and the worry was written all over their hearts.

I sat quietly, listening to them speak to me about Victoria and not knowing what to do next. I spent the day with Rebecca and Doreen, along with their family, and we went for a ride in Rebecca's car, as we went to visit Victoria's mother's house. We came up with an idea for me to gain information by reading Victoria's mother and being a plant in her home, known as John, a friend of the family.

Psychic Profiler The Real Deal

The drive seemed to go by in slow motion, as I observed a police vehicle just down the street a bit, keeping careful watch over the home of Victoria's mother. There were children playing in the front yard, riding bikes, and one enthusiastic young boy, jumping his bike on a homemade ramp in the driveway. His name was Daryn and he was so proud of his accomplishments by riding his bike fast to jump over that ramp. This brave young boy was Rebecca's nephew, who seemed to be lost in the fun of the day with a couple other kids from the block. It was a very different feeling going into Victoria's mother's house, as I noticed a gentleman sitting on the stairs, arms crossed with his head down, white T-Shirt and jeans, looking at the floor not sociable and not very attentive to us being there.

A very cold reception emanated from him, as he never attempted to raise his head at all to see who we were that entered the backdoor, into the kitchen area. I then noticed a lady, sitting at the kitchen table, typing on a laptop; she briefly looked up, saying hello to Rebecca and Doreen. I was introduced to her by Rebecca and told her name was Tara and that I was a friend of the family, which at this point she smiled at me.

She continued to browse on her laptop while Rebecca began discussing family matters with her. The only thing that stuck out in my mind, was the fact she lifted her head up from the laptop, only to complain about the police being in her home, looking at her coat in the closet down the long hall from the kitchen and the fact they took her computer from her. Seemed a bit odd to me, however, everyone grieves differently in circumstances that they were going through.

I noticed, also, prior to coming in that there was a backpack belonging to Victoria under the back porch, which Rebecca addressed with the mother, and it was said they put it there because of having beer in it or something to that affect. At one point a couple young teenage kids came from the living room, off to the right of the kitchen, down that long hallway as they then turned around, and went back into the living room. The entire time in the home, I was getting too many different reads on many things, for this was where Victoria lived and there was too much going on. It became something of uncomfortably numb, as I felt there is more here than meets the eye in this entire bring me into this home as a plant so-to-speak.

My focus was for Victoria, and I was reverting back in my mind to my sketches, notes, and then I started that so called "comparing" individuals with what I had written down that was given to Rebecca and the detectives. I had to stop for a brief moment, as my emotions were becoming the best of me; I totally understand how I have to separate these feelings for the betterment of getting down to the truth. We weren't long at this home before we again were off for a ride to see, if anything I had given in my impressions would pop out at me around the city.

During our slow, long drive, we discussed many matters concerning Victoria and family life. We talked about matters that affected the heart, knowing how the child living with her mother wasn't one Doreen or Rebecca approved of because of conditions and much more. It was very difficult listening to everything, but in the interim, while sitting in the passenger seat, I let it all sink in.

Psychic Profiler The Real Deal

These are stories that are now completely all over the internet about her home life with her mother, Tara and yet, there were more the public never knew, I was listening to real family vent the truth behind closed doors as they were very open and honest, loving people, wanting answers for their little Angel taken from them.

Not only were my feelings correct about Victoria's living, but the virtual seeing of behavioral attitudes, along with the disposition the people within Tara's home took, it truly created a foundation of a realization there must be more, I feel there is much more to this! It was like playing hide and seek, a try and find the answers, if you can situation, however, it was only a one sided venture and not of Victoria.

I was becoming entranced with all the outside interference of frustration, coming from every direction and in feeling this, it was normal to be human, realizing the love everyone has for this Angel missing. The actual drug abuse and use Tara was known for, as it too, is now public record, but knowing that the two who took Victoria, they had indeed, had some type of relationship or friendship with Tara, which would become another speculative direction everyone would slowly come to find out in the near future through the media. This was all discussed with me in our talks after leaving the house; it kept the mind sharp to everything going on as this case had many angles to it. There just seemed to be more than what meets the eye on everything. I had my reservations on many of the people within this case outside Rodney's family.

Things just didn't add up or the normal activity of an individual, who is supposed to be the protector of a child, yet had an entirely different outlook on things. Again, I tossed it up lightly as everyone grieves differently in situations like this!

What struck everyone at the time is, Tara never once left the house to look for Victoria and this, too, was brought up in conversation; however, Rodney, spent every waking moment in the public eye, searching for his beautiful little daughter, Victoria. He endlessly pounding the pavement, putting up posters, showing up for news conferences, speaking with authorities, the public and organized rally's for his daughter, day in and day out. This too, was also public knowledge and made the news many times. The lack of one and the endless effort of the other, it only made speculation run rampant in people's minds.

Everything we discussed in the car, we continued back at the family home. At one point, Rebecca asked me how I thought Victoria was hurt. My heart fell as I slowly gestured I heard two hits on the head while I took my fist and hit my other hand. It got extremely quiet for a moment as I gazed into Rebecca's tear filled eyes. I sat listening to much more that the public would cringe about and I finally spoke up gently to everyone there. I mentioned, if any of this information, they were telling me, was actually given to the police investigators, so they could utilize it in the investigation in finding Victoria. The room got quiet, everyone just looked at me, and I thought I said something out of turn, but that wasn't it at all.

Psychic Profiler The Real Deal

Without hesitation, Rebecca and Doreen, both, looked to each other and stressed they hadn't even thought of it. There wasn't a moment they considered to actually bring forth this type of information to the police.

Immediately, Doreen stood up from her chair, asking, if I would like to accompany them to the police station to offer up this information, which was indeed, very important for the investigating detectives. We eventually made it to the Police Station, to meet with Detective Brown, to discuss my findings and perhaps go over much detail as possible.

At the same time, Rodney, Victoria's father, was in taking a polygraph test, as this is a normal procedure in police work when there is a missing child or family member on any case. After his test, Rodney was shown to a room where we were waiting to speak with Detective Brown. Rebecca begins to introduce me to Rodney, being this was the first time I got to meet him that day. I could tell the frustration he was dealing with in the other room, taking a polygraph test isn't a pleasant ordeal whatsoever.

Detective Brown enters the room and was very cordial towards everyone, while Rebecca begins to speak to her on the findings that I had given to her. We went over many aspects of what I was seeing in my premonitions and the fact of being in film myself, which we discussed possibilities of rendering a different outlook for the grainy picture of a woman, leading Victoria away from the school she attended that day. My drawings were brought up as we reviewed the items of interest on the paper I sent Rebecca.

We were later escorted to the lobby, to wait while individually everyone gave a statement to Detective Brown, on what we were there for in offering more information concerning Victoria. As I sat in the lobby, speaking with Rebecca, you could sense many unanswered questions going through her mind and that of Doreen as well. Randi, Rebecca's husband was in giving his statement and time seem to go by slowly as we all anticipated each going in taking their turn.

The lobby was very quiet and the day was getting on when Rebecca turned to me, asking my thoughts on Rodney, her brother. I was taken back a bit by this; however, I just smiled and asked her, if she felt he had involvement in Victoria's disappearance? She looked me in the eyes directly and responded appropriately saying she didn't think so.

I knew she wanted to hear more on what I was thinking and feeling on him being there taking a polygraph. Rebecca is clearly a real thinker, someone who looks at the entire picture in life as this is how I felt about her. My answer to her settled her anxiety from everything going on that day at the Police Station.

I told her, her brother was a wholesome man, a solid guy, and that I knew he had nothing to hide whatsoever. I sensed after telling Rebecca this, her heart was put at ease because the man Rodney is, shines through in his character and perseverance. I honestly found him to be a straightforward individual that just wants answers to everything concerning his daughter. A real stand up fella with his heart on his sleeve and his heart with his beautiful little daughter Victoria.

Psychic Profiler The Real Deal

Rebecca looked me in the eyes and took my hand, smiling, this I knew was her confirmation she was looking for because don't forget, everyone was distraught, literally being torn up inside, and it didn't mean she was putting the blame on her brother, it was just the moment and that is all it was nothing more.

Time went by rather slow; there were periods where I got a chance to see the amount of activity going on within the Police Station as officers rushing in and out from the field. I commend the efforts of Law Enforcement add everyone involved as there were quick news updates out front where we could actually see this taking place while sitting in the lobby. A female spokeswoman in uniform would come out; addressing the press in what information they had at the time.

After everyone gave their statements to Detective Brown, the family and I left the Police Station and headed back to their home. We spent time talking about certain things as to our statements given and the day was coming to a close, so, I suggested I had better start on the road heading back to my family. Before I left, Rebecca asked, if I would contact Victoria or when she did indeed contact me at any time, could I ask her, if she was around the family, to prove she was with them. I smiled and agreed that I would indeed do this for them, how could I not. I love this family and we have become very close during this time. It just so happens to be that night, and as I was climbing into bed, I explained to my wife that I was going to reach out to Victoria to see if she answers me.

I spoke out loud saying, "Victoria, if you are here or you hear me, can you knock for me please?" It wasn't more than two seconds and there were five baby knocks on the wall behind my wife and I. Immediately, my wife pulled the covers over her head, slid over to me in the bed, and asked, "What was that?" I smiled saying, "That, that is Victoria!" My wife literally melted into my side in bed shaking.

I spoke up again and asked, "Victoria, could you show me something that only your dad or Rebecca would know that you are around them please?" Immediately, flashes of a girl a young lady wearing a ball cap was shown me. Then for some funny reason, a stuffed fox head that literally sat on top of that ball cap! None of this made any sense to me, but regardless, it was coming from Victoria and I jumped out of bed to start my sketching.

After compiling my sketching and information, I laid back down in bed content in what I had just received and thanked Victoria. My wife on the other hand, still shaken from everything that was taking place, was like glue to my hip, wanting to know what just happened in this exchange. The night was eventful to say the least and I couldn't wait until morning to call Rebecca and give her the information.

That phone call came quick and as I had Rebecca on the other end, I started explaining the night's events that took place. Once I started to talk about the girl with the ball cap and a stuffed fox head that sat on top of it, Rebecca gasped. She said, "She bought him that hat yesterday!" I sat for a moment and had to ask, "What hat are we talking about?" Rebecca replied, "She bought him a Fox Racing Hat!"

Psychic Profiler The Real Deal

Chills went down my spine, and up my arms, I just knew that this was a solid connection for the family; this is what they were waiting for. Now, I understand and this was very good validation, as they wanted to know, if Victoria was around them, a proof positive and in a huge Fox Hat way! I forwarded on my sketches to Rebecca via fax so they could have it as this was from Victoria.

A fair amount of time has passed, however, Rebecca and I continually stayed in contact throughout this period. One thing we discussed after the fact was how Victoria died. Rebecca wanted to know, exactly how Victoria met her fate. I sat for a moment on the phone with her and paused, knowing the next words out of my mouth weren't something I was really willing to give up. I looked into my left palm of my hand and with the motion of striking; I took my right hand making that motion like a hammer to the head. I mentioned I felt two strikes to the head, "Two blows to her head", I said. This loving family even invited my wife and me to her wedding that was going to take place. I felt totally honored from her sending us invitations.

During the course of staying in contact after our meetings in Woodstock, a break came, and the girl who was caught on camera, and that I profiled before they released this information to the public, was in custody and talking. The police were being tight lipped about this new discovery of having a suspect in custody other than releasing facts of her name only. We all held tight to this information, hoping something would come of it from the suspect. She seemed to be elusive in the beginning, as they took her up in the air in a helicopter searching for the area in question that she described.

This area was to be where her accomplice Michael Rafferty took Victoria's life. Victoria's body was discovered in that tree line, right by that big pile of rocks and wood, right off that laneway where all those horse and buggy drawn carriages went and right by the Mennonite village. It's so eerie, thinking about this and how accurate the description of everything was right there, right in front of us all.

Surveillance caught Terri McClintic, shopping at a local store, buying items that would be used in the death of Victoria. One of those items was a hammer, which McClintic and Michael Rafferty heinously took her life with. She bludgeoned Victoria's head with a hammer while her head was covered with garbage bags. This is as much as I want to speak of in the manner they took Victoria's life. They are animals beyond any conception and should be treated as such.

This still pains me today and every day I think of this family of Victoria's. As the trial for Michael Rafferty went forth and the verdict was rendered, we all waited anxiously. Guilty of murder! Rafferty will serve twenty five years in prison before he is eligible for parole (and let's all pray they never let the scumbag out). McClintic had previously pleaded guilty to first-degree murder and is serving a life sentence, two years prior. We went down to Woodstock once we learned of the guilty verdict as the family planned a balloon release for Victoria. It was a symbolization of letting her know and letting her go.
Rodney, Victoria's Dad and myself, posed for a fast photo at the final balloon release in Woodstock, as we said we love you Victoria and release her and the balloons into Heaven. That moment will always be a reminder for me personally of this beautiful family.

Psychic Profiler The Real Deal

After that night of the balloon release and being at home, things were exactly the way they were when Victoria first went missing. I was on the one couch exactly the same way sitting and my wife on the other with the kids sitting on the floor and laying in the chairs when out of the blue, there she was. She had a yellow flower and there were butterflies all around her. She walked right up to me and came into my arms. I started to cry and hugged her so tight, as there was silence in the room and not a word spoken. It lasted for about a minute, no more, and as fast as she appeared, she was gone. I looked over at my wife who was glaring at me, wondering what was going on and then I noticed my kids just staring, looking for an explanation of some sort.

I just looked up and closed my eyes, thanking her because this was her way of saying thank you to me. It was Victoria, coming once more to thank me, and I know the message behind this is for Rodney, Rebecca, Doreen and the family. She came to me without speaking a word, just hugged me, and in a symbolic way, handed me that yellow flower with all those butterflies around her.

God Bless You, Victoria! Angel Upon High!

Herbert Brewer Sr. & Herbert Brewer Jr.
Father Son Taken From Us

Active Law Enforcement Officer, Andy DeLay's Statement!

"In 2009, I was the host of a syndicated radio show in London, Kentucky called, Burning Rubber Radio. I was contacted by a local listener, who knew that I was a retired law enforcement officer, but wanted help about a fire that killed her father and brother 7 years prior. I was retired from a central Florida law enforcement agency and not certified as an officer in Kentucky; however, I told the lady that I would look into the matter as a courtesy.

The lady supplied me with documents of the investigation that was completed by the Laurel County Sheriff's Office and the State of Kentucky. After examining the investigation, two things were glaringly apparent to me.

Psychic Profiler The Real Deal

　　1. Two people were killed in a mobile home fire.

　　2. The investigation was botched and half-heartedly conducted.

　　It became apparent that simple rules of crime scene preservation and basic investigation skills were not adhered to during the arson investigation. The Sheriff's Office came to the conclusion that the fire was not suspicious and the deaths of the two men were accidental. My conclusion as a retired (And now again current) law enforcement officer, are quite different. The fire was set to cover up the murder of two healthy adult men, who were awake and fully mobile prior to the crime, inside of a small single-wide mobile home.

　　Forensic evidence gathered at the scene, reveals blunt trauma to the skulls of the two men. The State Fire Marshal explains this as the result of the intense heat of the fire. My investigation revealed the fire was not hot or intense enough to cause heat induced intracranial explosion of the skull; in fact, the skulls were not exploded, they were imploded or crushed due to blunt trauma. There was also accelerant found at the scene by the State Fire Marshall.

　　Presented with the facts collected by the Sheriff's Office and State Fire Marshall, I had a reasonable suspicion, these men were murdered. I told the victim's family to contact the Sheriff's Office about my findings. The victim's family approached the then Sheriff, about the questionable investigation of the incident. The small town Sheriff quickly excused the family's concerns and actually referred to them as, "Crazy". I then directed the family to the State Police. The State Police declined to open the investigation; instead, they referred the family back to the Laurel County Sheriff's Office.

The family had effectively hit a dead end and now, a person or persons were about to get away with murder. I could not walk away from this, knowing there was at least a reasonable doubt that the men were murdered. I met with the Sheriff about the incident, showing him why I thought there was doubt that the investigation was conducted properly and why I believed the men were murdered. The Sheriff dismissed my concerns, referred to the family as crazy, and became quite confrontational with me as I was shown the door to his office. This only raised more questions to me about the incident. Why is this Sheriff, becoming defensive and confrontational? Why is he dismissing a law enforcement officer with many years of experience, when in fact, the Sheriff was never a law enforcement officer prior to his current term of office? This at minimum deserved a second look, but the Sheriff would have nothing of it.

I was a paranormal investigator with the TAPS group, Kentucky Shadow Chasers at the time. I have heard of the good work done by Psychic Forensic Investigators, and I happened to follow the work of one... Robbie Thomas. I contacted Robbie and informed him of what I had and then put him in touch with the family.

Robbie agreed that something was amiss. Enter, Robbie Thomas into the investigation. Things were about to become very interesting. Robbie arrived in Kentucky and reviewed the forensic evidence. Robbie, the family and I, visited the scene of the fire. Robbie, felt strongly that these men had been robbed and killed before the house had been set afire.

Psychic Profiler The Real Deal

Robbie and I, now, began to do some old fashioned police work. His intuition, coupled with my investigation, began to develop several suspects. Questioning of the suspects was even more fruitful, as stories didn't match and people became very nervous. It was as if, Robbie and I had turned the lights on in a dirty kitchen and the roaches were sent scrambling.

Robbie and I continued the investigation to the point that I actually developed probable cause to arrest a person of interest in this case. If I were at work and investigating the crime as a on the job law enforcement officer, I would have made an arrest. It was now a sure thing. Due to Robbie's intuition and my investigation of those leads, we now had a confirmed crime. I brought these facts and conclusions to both the Sheriff and the State Police. Again, we were stone-walled.

It has come to my attention, in the years since we investigated this, the person of interest had died. On his deathbed, he gave his confession. He murdered the men and set fire to the home, just as Robbie and I concluded. Without the use of Robbie's intuition, the family would have never had closure. The Laurel County Sheriff's Office has since come under new leadership and Sheriff, and thankfully the old guard is gone. I do not credit myself with the closure of this case. I credit the God given gift that Robbie Thomas possesses, as the reason the person who committed this heinous crime, did not go to the grave hiding their secrets, but instead, let a family continue on with their life with closure." -Andy DeLay, Active Law Enforcement Officer, Kenneth City Sheriff's Office, Florida, United States

I received an email that started this entire case off, with a request to appear on Officer DeLay's radio show, Burning Rubber. The show was to include the work I do with Law Enforcement and that of the research within the Paranormal Field. We quickly began discussing various cases that Officer DeLay had followed me on and that of our meeting at a couple conventions on the same topic in 2007 and 2008 in Kentucky and West Virginia. Officer DeLay began discussing a current case that he was involved with, helping a family on a double homicide.

He asked me one question after the brief introduction of his involvement in this case and that was, "If I could pick up anything on the case and who all were involved?" I paused for a brief moment, searching for the answers to the question that just took me off guard, as I didn't realize I was going to be put on the spot, live on a syndicated radio program. In the serious tone the show quickly took, I knew Andy, Officer DeLay, was looking for some insight from a Psychic who has worked many cases in the past, so I gave information that was coming into me as requested by him live on air. The visions were rampant, steady, and descriptive all while relaying certain information that caught the interest of Andy.

I spoke up, mentioning there were three individuals involved in this terrible crime, also certain particular aspects to the crime, which weren't made public in any news agency or media, prior to me going on his show. Andy paused for a moment, and then remarked that indeed, this was the suspicion he had that the family would most certainly be interested in my findings in that short segment of the show.

Psychic Profiler The Real Deal

Shortly after the show was finished, Andy spoke to me off air and was taken back by my visions of the entire case outline thus far, which in turn, he mentioned that I must come to Kentucky to assist in this case, to help bring closure for this family he had discussed with me. The poignant, crucial impressions I gave over the air and now that we were off air, we reviewed them with further details, which only solidified Andy's desire to have me help investigate this crime. It was soon after this show, Andy put me in touch with the family, who after hearing the show themselves, were astounded with the impressions I gave, which I had no prior knowledge of this case.

The Brewer family, what a beautiful collective of souls they are and through phone calls, arrangements of me coming to Kentucky, and all the emails, I was starting to truly see how much love this family has for one another. The outpouring of seeking the help they so needed was evident, for the justice they sought wasn't being met from an investigative point of view. They were left hanging with no resolve or course of action from the local Sheriff's office. Something was creeping up my spine, knowing, could this be neglect, forgetfulness, or just plain laziness on the part of the investigators on this investigation.

My heart went out to them and I knew within myself I had to assist, I did indeed need to fly to Kentucky to be on the front lines once more in a high profile case. Things just seem to work out better when I'm in person, on the front lines assisting. It gives a completely different perspective doing so along with the presence it lends much more to the active work at hand.

There was something amiss on every aspect of this case that integral technical points, either got overlooked or just the devastation of this entire case got lost in the initial investigations, due to emotional override. I had my reservations on many points as my visions or impressions, if you will, were giving me a different outlook on everything thus far that I have come to know in this heinous crime. Without a doubt, from the onset of being asked a simple question live on a radio show, broadcasted worldwide and coming up with three suspects, pertinent information not known to the public, someone indeed was guiding me for this family so they could find the answers, which weren't given to them during their time of need.

"We called in a Psychic Profiler, Robbie Thomas. We heard him on a radio program of a friend of ours and he was talking and describing our dad and brothers case. This was before we had contacted him to come down here. He said, there were three attackers and he described details that my niece didn't know about yet, but some of us kids did because we were sworn to secrecy in order to keep from damaging the case. Thank you, Robbie, for believing us when the local police had turned their back on our case.

Your help in getting the answers we were looking for is greatly appreciated by the friends and family of Herbert Brewer and Herbie Brewer Jr. Although we didn't receive the conviction we were hoping for, you found witnesses who were willing to tell us what they saw that night and it helped us to find a sense of closure that we had been seeking for so long. The justice that Dad and Herbie deserve will be dealt out in the next life if not this one."

Psychic Profiler The Real Deal

Friends Forever, in this life and the next.

Alene Brewer Spurlock

Robbie Thomas at the site where the murders took place with the Brewer family members.

I met up with Andy (Officer DeLay), and we went out to meet the Brewer family in the picture above, at their father's property where the terrible crime was committed. This family, with so much God fearing love in their hearts, needed answers for what had happened to them and their loved ones. It felt like someone was deliberately keeping them from the truth, the honest truth of what took place because of something that went wrong in the investigations.

It wasn't so much impropriety on the part of the investigators, as it was more of a miscue in what to look for or who to look at. Undue diligence in fortitude towards asserting proper crime scene investigation, also that of an ignorance to know better in sifting through the intricate, detailed surface of what was so evident from the beginning. I figured the rested upon their laurels, giving the fact assumptions without proper analysis was conducted in collecting evidence or broadening the investigative powers.

After our discussions with the family on what they knew of the circumstances, Andy and I, started to formulate our plan of investigation on what we came to know in the case. Our thoughts were threefold, wanting to contact the suspects for possible interaction, organize our path of investigating the whereabouts of each on that dreadful day, and relive every moment leading up to that point by doing what each suspect said they were doing on that day. We felt within the branches of each statement, lie substantial bookmarkers, which would evidently lead us to a direction in finding the missing link in the case. I had my visions that were backed by solid Police work from an outstanding investigator and now, our work was about to begin!

We decided to critically pace off the length of the winding road to see what the one suspect was saying could be justified. Timeline was essential, for this was given to us by yet another individual who was harboring the truth or accessory if you will, to the fact of this murder. In no conceivable thought whatsoever, what he was feeding us was right, it didn't fit the profile of time, distance and deliberate thought.

We ended up at the residence a quarter of a mile down the road, which was completely blocked, not only from the topography of the landscape, but the large, dense, tree line, which literally hovered over the house on the property, making it impossible to be able to view the fire or smoke pouring into the air that night. This only lent suspicion on the suspect's testimony making this easier for us to pursue the truth, seeking justice in this case.

Psychic Profiler The Real Deal

There was a lull in the conversation, as Officer DeLay stood thirty feet from where I stood, with one of the daughters of the murdered gentleman. In a very stern tone, Detective DeLay shouts out, "I can pull my sidearm faster than you can pull that trigger on that shotgun!" I glanced over at Andy, wondering what was he saying, and who was he saying this to!

A cold sweat beaded on my forehead, as I glanced through the trees, only to see an old woman, pointing a rather large gun directly at me. Things got very interesting from this point! After careful examination of the situation at hand, Officer DeLay was able to calm the circumstances and the older lady, holding a shotgun, returned to her home. She was plenty upset at the fact we were investigating her son and friend of the family, which she embellished the moment by stressing we were encroaching onto her property. Nothing further from the truth, however, this would prove not to be the only strange encounter from this lady as the day progressed; we were in for a treat.

As Officer DeLay finished his calculations, and report on the actual visual statement given from one of the three suspects, and his cohort, we returned up the road to the scene where the heinous crime was committed.

We asked the family to remain behind on their property while we could conduct part of the investigation without impedance because time was of the essence. What we didn't expect, was frequent drive-bys, by this older woman from the encounter previous just moments ago. Yes, it became a heightened awareness for all while she would drive radically by us at a high rate of speed, as we all watched standing on the Brewer family property.

It seems as the full moon was high in the sky, the crazies do indeed crawl out from under the rocks so-to-speak! It was learned later that night, during one of our visits with the Brewer family, the lady who was out to intimidate us, was pulled over and drugs were found in the trunk of the car. See, the entire area and even the county over are seeping with Methamphetamine Labs, and many other drugs run rampant throughout this county, making for a very disturbing situation in this entire area for the folks that live there.

With time ticking away and the night coming to an end on the first night, Officer DeLay and I, returned back to the hotel and to the boardroom area, to discuss our disposition for the day. There were many things still a miss during our office time, discussing this case as to the timeline, placement of people and broken stories. During earlier that day, I suggested we should purchase colored markers and Bristol board, so we could profile the case in an outline, to present to our leading suspect of choice, knowing it would catch him off guard. I decided to begin, by giving my impressions of suspect #3, who we felt would be the go to person and the weakest link of the three in this crime.

It proved to be the right move and in turn much came from this as we progressed throughout the night, laying out our plan to get information to incriminate those involved. I began by giving my psychic impressions of his character and behavior before, during, and after the crime at hand.

Psychic Profiler The Real Deal

I laid out his personality, what his role was during this murder on one Bristol board, and on a second board, I projected his disposition while these murders took place with the other two suspects. It left no room for error nor did it open up any holes for the suspect to see a chance to redirect any suspicion whatsoever.

Both, Officer DeLay and I, after many hours on the first day, found ourselves, looking at a completed profile of a suspect that we knew would crack under pressure. The next day would prove to be a test of wills, as we now were faced with a shortened timeline that needed expedition on getting facts and a possible confession. We had our work cut out for ourselves, but we had determination in this case.

Morning came early, in fact, it was just a few hours ago we had just finished up with the profiling and going over all our gathered investigation notes. There was no time to waste and no rest for the wicked, as those who were involved in this crime, were finding out that I was in town, and working with Officer DeLay. We made plenty of office visits with the Sheriff and his detective at the time, which things seemed hugely obscure in us digging for facts.

I was forewarned by Officer DeLay that the entire case was completely botched, as much in the way of evidence was not given a proper look, and disregarded in every way possible. The family wasn't getting their questions answered, as it became more of a run-around they felt, and this was expressed to me thoroughly in the dismay they had. They felt cheated on every turn of this case, and here is where we needed to dig deeper to uncover everything, starting from scratch.

I felt a cover-up of disregard and incompetence that smudged every aspect of this case while speaking with the Sheriff's office, nevertheless, aside from Officer DeLay looking at me with a disgusted look on his face, we pressed onward to find the answers that were hidden in shadows from the Sheriff's office.

We decided to place a couple of phone calls directly to the suspects themselves, inviting them to meet with us to discuss various intricate details in the case. The main suspect, reluctant to grant us a meeting, suggested we come to his house, but he couldn't guarantee our safety if we did. He played cat and mouse with us several times that day during calls we placed to him. His daily activity changed drastically during the time I was in town, working with Officer DeLay, which in essence is a sign of avoidance knowing we were on to him.

The suspect #2, John, well, we learned his whereabouts, which in light of his background, suited his character completely. He was arrested for beating and robbing an individual and had a nice cell with a view! Now, we thought, if we could get to him before Ronnie, the main suspect, we might be able to make a deal of sorts for his cooperation in nailing the main suspect.

We already learned Ronnie was desperately trying to contact our go-to-guy, as he had built a fear factor, which seemed to have a huge bearing on him. We had to move and move fast, if we wanted to beat this ring leader to the punch, and get our questions answered as to who, where, what and when. It definitely became a thinking motive in achieving our goal, for Ronnie was manipulative and cunning.

Psychic Profiler The Real Deal

Regardless of our desperate intentions, once again, bad luck had an upper hand; however, Bobby agreed to meet with us at the end of his driveway for a few moments, to discuss the circumstances surrounding the case. We now knew we had our in, our decisive opportunity to squeeze information from the weakest link, and it was just moments away. We hurried over to Bobby's residence with bated breath, and the anxiety of knowing, this was a make or break moment. Both, Officer DeLay and I, were anxious as two kids in a candy store, looking at all the treats eye level, knowing they're at our reach.

Finally, here we are, heart pounding, anxious, but cool as a cucumber, as we wait for Bobby, to make that long walk down that winding driveway from his house that sat way back on a large property. As he slowly approached, his demeanor and the way he carried himself, fit the profile I wrote up on the Bristol boards exactly. Just a lanky, nerdy looking kid, one that would be the grunt of a group of kids you'd expect to be mischievous, but not to be mistaken, still one that would most definitely be part of a gang of murderers most certainly.

He greeted both Andy and me, but the way he titled me, set me back a bit. I shook his hand and from that alone, it told me so much more, as I seen right through his ploy to play the disadvantaged, wounded child. He referred to me as, "Mr. FBI!" I knew these were words of choice from the main suspect, Ronnie, which were feathered through his thoughts and words.

Nevertheless, I went along with it because I knew from that moment that very moment, Bobby couldn't speak for himself, which left him in a vulnerable position, and a huge disadvantage with me, as I was about to read him, and tell him exactly what I thought.

Andy discussed with me prior that, if a moment had arisen where this kid was going to go beyond playing us for stupid, we were going to become the, "good cop/bad cop" scenario. Well, he showed his true colors and Andy had about all he was going to take. "You want to play it like that do you?" Andy spoke up in a very serious tone and opened the side door to the vehicle we were in, pulling out the two Bristol boards, placing them on the back of the vehicle. He turned to Bobby saying, "Have a read of that! That is exactly what he (referring to me), profiled you as. That's exactly you and what you did! I know that's you and exactly who you are, don't play games with me!"

Andy wasn't about to let this coward slip through our fingers and he wasn't about to put up with any more of Bobby's antics. Andy once again, reiterates, challenging this young man standing in front of us who was starting to crumble quickly. "You know you were there! You did this and everything on these boards point to you! Doesn't it?"

Bobby went quiet, just staring at everything written before him and his eyes were as big as golf balls, with a dumbfounded look on his face. He didn't move or flinch, he just kept staring in bewilderment, and I knew what was going through his mind. He was wondering, how the hell I came up with him completely, placing it in front of him to see in reality, it was the clarity of it all that awestruck moment and it set him back!

Psychic Profiler The Real Deal

His breath was becoming quicker, developing a very nervous twitch that followed with consecutive involuntary touching of his nose and arm over and over. His poster took a whole different stance, leaving him shifting his weight from one leg to the other often. Andy was taking a great position on the line of questioning, putting Bobby at a huge disadvantage, leaving him completely confused in what to say next. At this point, Andy hands me the cassette recorder and I moved closer to Bobby, playing the good cop in this theater of inquisition!

Andy, acting frustrated threw his hands into the air, saying he'd had it, and if I had anything to say, to go right ahead and talk to Bobby. I glanced over at Bobby as he went white as a sheet and started to become sheltered within his responses as they weren't fluent or concise. He kept looking back at the house back on the hill, down that long driveway, which I kept a keen eye on, as I felt someone like Ronnie himself was watching from the distance. I had to act fast and jump on that moment while we had Bobby nervous as a rat in a cage.

Here's my opportunity to enter the mindset of an individual who was part of a murder, which wasn't my first go around doing this and the time seemed so fitting. I held the recorder directly in front of Bobby and didn't ask him, but told him that I knew he was there that night, I knew he took part in something so terrible that he should look for forgiveness by cooperating with us. I explained to him, I knew he didn't start the fire or hit the two gentlemen with the baseball bat or cut them with a knife, but he was there and seen what exactly occurred.

I wanted him to cave fast, I felt his being, crumbling before me and it was just a matter of time. The taste of victory over the evilness was just at my grasp, yet it was totally up to Bobby to concede, giving us what we knew already. It had to come from his mouth, from his thoughts that he was trying so hard to conceal in order for us to have a viable true confession of what took place.

He was reluctant in shaking his head no, but again, I knew he wanted to say yes, as his head at this time hung low and he couldn't look me in the eyes. I reiterated my line of statements, more-so than questioning him, up until the point I told him that I saw him there, as Ronnie, and John, killed both Herbert Sr., and Herbert Jr. Suddenly, his verbalizing came in the method of nodding of his head, yes! He did this twice, without actual verbalization, and then I spoke up, asking him to speak clearly so it could be recorded.

He kept calling me, "Mr. FBI man!" I knew I was getting to him because I hate bull-shitters! Oh, and as everyone knows, I'm just that way, and I let it be known. Anyways, as I looked at him, I said, "I think you're full of shit! Now, don't get me wrong, but the last time I checked, shit goes downhill.

Are you that shit?" His response that kept coming up, you guessed it! "Mr. FBI man", and he'd go into his slow southern drawl of an answer. So, I told him while looking at the Officer DeLay, "I got you and you know it! You're going down fast!" I was clasping my right hand in a fist. "Come on Bobby, you can't fool me", I kept telling myself. I had to stay cool and be his friend, slow it down a bit so I can get him to relax and confess.

Psychic Profiler The Real Deal

He finally raised his head, looking me directly in the eyes and you could see it in his face, he knew there was no way to avoid the truth any longer. He said, "Yes!" Officer DeLay and I, looked at each other and knew, we got the truth from a kid who was so scared that he couldn't hide it anymore. The defining moment of getting that confession, which was so gratifying is in the knowing that it came from explaining what we knew, without wavering one bit. It came from the hard work and diligence of working this case so hard, for so many hours without hesitation. It came because we knew Bobby would cave! On the drive back to the boardroom, we were beside ourselves in jubilation, knowing, we just got this kid to acknowledge the complete situation of this crime.

The excitement was bursting with different emotions of elation and now, we have to get a hold of the Brewer family, we have to let them know how it the entire situation went down, and that we had Bobby. Andy contacts Alene (Herbert Sr's daughter), explaining what we just went through and the outcome of that meeting.

Everyone was ecstatic for the most part, however, there was more work to be done with the other two suspects in this case. We wanted to solidify what Bobby told us, with the corroboration of Ronnie's statements, if he'd cooperate and meet with us as well. Tension was building most certainly, with the prospects of Ronnie in our sights now and him feeling the pressure of this case. We knew deep in our gut, Ronnie would either give a confession now or give himself up entirely because we got to Bobbie.

Word got out to Ronnie, and we were pleasantly surprised he wanted to speak with us by phone. Andy placed a call to his house where he lived with his mother, catching him in perfect timing. Ronnie was one for being very elusive since this small town was a busybody of knowledge when something goes down, everyone knows everyone's business. Ronnie's demeanor was one of less appreciation because of the deceptive tone, and outright toying with us to visit him. He more-or-less dared us to come to his driveway to question him, almost like a charade of cat and mouse that he was enjoying, knowing we just spoke with Bobby. Our second prospect was John, however, John was incarcerated for a crime he committed earlier that week, which left us at a slight disadvantage.

This didn't detour us whatsoever, as Andy came up with a thought of letting on, we were going to visit John in jail before Ronnie could get to him, and we'd fake the fact we spoke with John already to Ronnie.

Andy explained this over the phone to the less cooperative, annoying, ringleader, and a lull in the conversation took place for a brief moment, until Ronnie decided, he had enough and hung up the phone. I really just wanted to grab this murderer by the neck and beat it out of him, but I know the feelings of doing this would interfere in our work at hand, so cool heads prevailed. This slim of a kid, who was so conniving, evil in every respect, had a disposition of manipulation of so many people. He had people scared of him, scared of the fact this sick individual was a very loose cannon, and we needed to put an end to his tyranny in this small town.

Psychic Profiler The Real Deal

Andy explained John rolled over on him, wanting to tell us the entire story of what took place, putting Ronnie as the main character in this crime. I think Ronnie shit his pants to-say-the-least, at that very moment and made haste to get to the jail to speak with John. It wasn't long before we also heard back from Bobby, which he now, had a change of heart in his story that had more than three sides to it. Either way, we still had that confession on tape, as Bobby was running scared, as he was well aware from Andy explaining to him, how much time he would be serving in prison for accomplice to murder!

With the perplexing situation heating up, and becoming clearer, we pieced everything together, getting ready to present the Sheriff's office with what we had. They say put the pressure on and watch them squirm! Well, if you were an audience of watchers, you would have witnessed some of the weirdest behavior from some stupid criminals ever.

Regardless of the extracurricular activities stirring within this small town from the obvious, we stayed steadfast to our convictions of gathered evidence and that confession from Bobby. We had them running scared, and then from out of nowhere, back at the property of Herbert Sr., a lady shows up apologizing for the actions of Ronnie, the main suspect in the case. This took us back; however, we kept quiet and just listened to whatever she had to offer in information about Ronnie. It became very apparent from the stories this lady had about Ronnie, we were dealing with a psychopath, someone who was deranged beyond comprehension.

He was a ticking time bomb that, if given another opportunity, would indeed commit this crime again with another family, or his very own. A strange turn of events was about to unfold, which only lent to the credibility of our case at hand. It seems, Ronnie's "MO", was exactly that of what transpired in this case from previous happenings within his own family. Both, Andy and I, weren't overly surprised, but in all the same, we were pleasantly surprised because the fact of the actions of setting the fire and stolen goods from this crime was exactly what he had done to his own mothers' home. The only difference was, Ronnie didn't commit murder, or perhaps in the stroke of luck, no one was in his mothers' home to become a victim of his criminal activity. As the night came to a close on this day of investigations, we had expedited meetings for the next day with the Sheriff's office, to divulge the information we had collected.

We were sitting pretty well in a position of getting a warrant sworn out for arrest, and having the three brought in for justice from this case, as the confession alone, placed all three on the property at the time of the murders.

Things were looking good, as Officer Delay collected and organized all his notes, I had my notes of much in the way that would be new leads for getting that sworn warrant, but and yes, there always seems to be a "but" doesn't there? This is something when everything seems to be going too good, we started to think, "No, don't do this, don't do this to us!"

Psychic Profiler The Real Deal

Next day rolls around, and we're set for these meetings with the Sheriff with everything we have to give him. We arrive early enough and to our surprise, the Sheriff was now, pushing us off onto his investigator on the case. This wasn't how things were supposed to be going down, nor did we agree to meet with an investigator who really didn't have much knowledge of the case. Nevertheless, as things will happen, we had no other choice, but to present our findings to the man who stood in front of us, as he invited us into his office.

Right from the moment this gentleman introduced himself to us, as the lead investigator, and the case was passed over to him from the Sheriff, you could just tell things started to really go downhill from here. Andy looked to me with a real sour look on his face, as we knew, we knew the railroading was about to begin. Andy whispered to me as we entered the office of this investigator, "Remember what I told you in the beginning, botched investigation!"

All I could do is bite my tongue, going along with what was about to take place. However, I'm not that type of guy, I'm not one for letting things go so easily, especially when I know the shenanigans were about to begin. The investigator loved the determination we had, and when we passed him the cassette tape of the confession of Bobby, he took it in his hand, placing it on his desk without a second glance. I looked to Andy and that was a huge sign that this wasn't going too far, or even getting a second glance. With everything presented that without a doubt constituted getting a warrant to be sworn out, it got brushed aside, and was taken very lightly by the investigator.

The investigator made mention that the case was closed because of it being an accident, and nothing further could, or would convince him otherwise. This didn't sit well with me, especially the tone and attitude he displayed. We mentioned the tape, and the fact of the confession, to which he said he would consider this, and call Bobby in to review it. We sat a bit longer, waiting, as Bobby showed up, only to be taken into a room alone with this investigator. About an hour transpired, and finally, the door swung open, with the investigator approaching us, stating that the tape had nothing on it.

Both, Andy and I, looked bewildered because we reviewed everything prior to going to the Sheriff's office, and everything was just as it should be. The investigator insisted that there was nothing whatsoever that would insist anything otherwise and that he wouldn't be furthering along the case.

However, if we wanted, he had a stack of cases that he'd be more than happy to hand over to us to assist in, finding closure to. I looked at this guy who was playing us for fools, and thought to myself, "This guy is on the take obviously from Bobby and the others as they dealt Meth. What a son of a bitch! Who does he think he's playing with!" Someone was in the back of someone's pocket that is most certain. I spoke up, and as I do, I was straightforward saying, "It's not the last you'll see or hear of me, or Officer DeLay because this is far from being closed." He just smiled with a real quirky smirk on his face and said, "We'll see!" Can you say, "Dirty-Pool!? Dirty Cop!" Oh hell ya!

Psychic Profiler The Real Deal

We knew it too, but all we could do is work double hard, pushing onward to convince the Sheriff through the media, and a possible meeting with him. See, the Sheriff was all talk, and very little walk, as he made promises that he just didn't keep.

A real man of his word, or like I told Andy, "A wordless man!" Bobby walked out of that Sheriff's office very shaken, knowing we were still there, watching, and I spoke up saying, "Don't get too comfortable, I know…we know! I got you, Bobbie!"

As time went on during my stay to assist, Andy and I had our last day sitting at a diner, drawing up reports, and final statements from our investigations. It was maddening, knowing the local Sheriff office, who botched this crime, weren't going to look at it in a different light, just because they didn't want to tarnish their reputation. What a crock of shit! These good ole boys were playing dirty cards because they knew, they knew exactly the truth, but it ran deeper.

The thing is as well, we had fire officials who also stated, these two men did not die from fire, and that the enormous frontal cranial indentation on Herbert Jr., was indeed created from a trauma blow to the head, by something like a baseball bat. Perhaps it was the baseball bat they found near his body, after they put the fire out. The ignition from the fire was indeed set by a flammable liquid, which again that, too, was close to the two men in a gas can. Too many variables, too many circumstances, a confession from the weakest link, the ringleader running scared, knowing we were on to him and so much more.

You remember me speaking of a knife being used in this heinous crime, and as I read for the family on the property of Herbert Sr., I told them, I know the knife was still on that property, but I couldn't put my finger on it, where it would be. Well, I got a phone call many months later from Alene, Herbert Sr.'s daughter, and they found a very large knife, hidden in the tool shed, behind the trailer that was set ablaze in the death of the two men. Interesting!

See, the two men were cut up bad from a knife that also contributed to their death, but once again, the Sheriff's office reluctantly denied looking at the knife for DNA, or considering it as a possible murder weapon. This loving family, all these beautiful people I had the opportunity to meet, and try to help in their quest to find the truth, were not given the slightest in the chance to find resolve from the Sheriff's office, yet they hung onto the hope of a Psychic and a Law Enforcement Officer, who did everything they could for them.

Oh, we knew, we all did after finding all that evidence, confession, and so much more, however, corruptness ran through the veins of a botched investigation that for the sake of a reputation, there was no second chance. In the end, as I found out as time dissipated, there were those who were involved, taking their own lives. I said that karma would come collecting her due, and she showed up with both hands wide open for those who committed this terrible crime. As my colleague, Andy (Officer DeLay) said, "They'll get theirs in time because time doesn't forget!" It never forgot and came collecting the debt it was owed.

Psychic Profiler The Real Deal

It was learned, and through the statement at the beginning of this chapter on this case by Officer DeLay that Ronnie, the ringleader, who was so selfishly living a life of taking and taking, found out the hard way. Karma and it is a shame that everything happened the way it did, and for what, for what did it profit this individual to take two lives, claim belongings from Herbert Sr. and Herbert Jr., and steal loved ones away from a beautiful family who didn't deserve this.

Ronnie ended up taking his life, which I can only sense he had a very hard time dealing with what he had done in his life to this family and much more. Officer DeLay mentions he confessed on his deathbed to doing these murders. Apparently, the voices in his head of the two he killed were ringing out injustice loud and clear. I told Ronnie this on the phone, that they would seek him out, they would want what he took from their family and he better be prepared to see the consequences of his actions.

He laughed in a way that admitted I was right and he knew it, it only took a matter of time of him taking his own life by his own hand. Karma, hell yah! Something his souls will have to pay over and over for however long God teaches him his mistakes. Let's hope he asked for forgiveness in doing so. I know from speaking to the family, they forgive because it is the right thing to do in order for them to move on in life, and love of God. It's not so much of who was right in this case, as it is the finding of the truth and resolve. The family has closure now, knowing, and are moving onward in their lives. May God Bless them and everyone involved. God Bless Herbert Sr. and Herbert Jr., may they rest in peace...Amen!

At the request of Rosalie Brewer, she wanted the Serenity Prayer to be put in after this chapter. I strongly agree, it is fitting!

God, give me grace to accept with serenity
The things that cannot be changed,
Courage to change the things
Which should be changed,
And the Wisdom to distinguish
The one from the other.
Living one day at a time,
Enjoying one moment at a time,
Accepting hardship as a pathway to peace,
Taking, as Jesus did,
This sinful world as it is,
Not as I would have it,
Trusting that You will make all things right,
If I surrender to Your will,
So that I may be reasonably happy in this life,
And supremely happy with You forever in the next.
Amen.

Much love goes out to the Brewer family…
God Bless them all!

Psychic Profiler The Real Deal

Paige Birgfeld Murder Case

(Ret. Sgt. Cliff Christ's Report/Notes On Case)

P.B. (Paige Birgfeld) Investigation Notes:

We contacted R.T. (Robbie Thomas), to assist in locating the remains of P.B. and or, to give any insight to her whereabouts in this case. Upon contacting R.T., I advised him in the capacity I wished him to assist in and could he be of help to this investigation at hand. Everything within these findings and report, were not made public or did R.T. have any prior knowledge of said crime, investigation, or any of the facts in the case, before or during I requested his assistance.

R.T. stated based on his remote viewing that:

1. The suspect he envisioned, was a man who worked as a mechanic, which worked on camping trailers, RV's and still works in that type of environment.

2. He makes mention of a name, (Les) like Lester. Also states he is in fact the killer who was involved with P.B. disappearance in this case.

3. R.T. states the killer still has the murder weapon and keeps it as a trophy, "possibly a screwdriver". He makes mention of a stabbing motion to her head area with this type of instrument and it being the cause of her death.

4. R.T. includes that the individual to him, still visits the location of the remains frequently. Almost like guarding the area of where P.B. would be found.

5. Remains are located, exactly where R.T. envisioned. Just off the roadway, between "quarter horse" ranches or by horse signs along the roadway. These were in his sketches he faxed to us prior to investigating.

6. P.B. remains were indeed located by water as R.T. had also included in his findings.

7. R.T. drew a sketch of the surrounding area that included a dried up creek bed area. The demographics of the drawings were indicative to the surroundings of where P.B. remains were found.

8. R.T. stated that the deceased remains to him are in a "fetal" position, possibly sitting in a shallow grave placed there by suspect in question (Site #1).

9. Remains were under or by a tree, in or around that area not far from the roadway as indicated by R.T.

10. Remains to R.T. are overlooking a dried bed creek, where evidence of foul play would be found and items of interest would be discovered.

11. R.T. includes that her remains had been moved at least once, from original crime scene and would be found in a second crime scene that would be discovered.

12. R.T. later stated, during our search that the remains had been moved due to investigation pressure from Law Enforcement and my investigative team.

Review of suspected abduction area

The area is a dirt and scrub parking area, where victim's car was burned and an unloaded gun found (gun was registered to suspect).

Psychic Profiler The Real Deal

Observations

1. Area shows recent fire damage from fire being purposely set.

2. Discovered that the area is less than 50 yards from suspect's place of employment.

3. Area is easily missed when driving by as it is out of view.

Suspects place of employment

The area is across the street from the abduction site, but cannot be seen from the business entrance. This was hidden from view.

We sent two undercover agents inside, posing as potential customers to ask a few questions. Agents attempted to locate suspects workstation, but left after being confronted by the said suspect. Suspect appeared to be somewhat nervous and apprehensive to the encounter with the two agents within his workplace, thus began tracking agents every move. Before we, (agents), left the location, we observed the suspect leaving work quickly and in a very suspicious manner.

Suspects Residence

We left his place of employment, heading for the suspects residence. Upon arrival, we discovered a small compact car occupied by a male driver, parked at the end of the street. We could not ascertain positively, if it was the suspect or not. The area was quite devoid of any foot or vehicle traffic. After taking several photos, we decided to leave the area and search areas that fit R.T's description. As we vacated the area, we discovered that the suspicious vehicle was following us.

We did conclude at this time that the driver was the suspect. We made several last minute turns and concluded he was tailing us. I then made several backtrack maneuvers and lost the suspect.

Search Area #1- The Desert

Although this area did not fit R.T's description, the outer perimeter did. This area had also been searched previously by the Mesa County Sheriff's Office. Our search found no evidence at the time. However, we made note of it as a possible search area for further investigation.

Search Area #2- Hwy 50/32rd

This area was where P.B's purse and other belongings were found on the side of the road.

1. Spiral searched the immediate area. No trace evidence found at this particular time.

2. Expanded search to one mile from intersection. Nothing matching R.T's description matched/no trace evidence found during this part of the investigation.

Search area #3- Whitewater to Delta

This area fit R.T's description on all points. We searched and probed numerous areas along Hwy 50 and numerous side roads.

1. We located a partially filled in hole in an area fitting R.T's description. It was located by a horse ranch and was overlooking a creek, exactly like he stated and in his sketches.

Psychic Profiler The Real Deal

Here also in this area we found a woman's blouse, something of polka dots and light in color. It looked to be torn from someone's body and was very close to the vicinity of that half dug hole. (Note: Paige Birgfeld was known for wearing such articles of clothing that matched this description that we found.)

2. There were signs that someone had been there on numerous occasions, again, like R.T. explained about the suspect visiting area to guard or check up on. This does fit R.T's statement that this was the visiting area for the suspect and was later moved due to current investigative pressure at the time.

3. We expanded the search further south towards Delta County, due to numerous R.T. Description "hits", the area was deemed too large to search and most searches were hindered by inaccessible areas or private property.

All areas that were searched resulted in nothing found at the time of investigating.

After Comments

R.T. Stated we were correct on the "Whitewater hole". He also stated that we were within 2 miles of her remains when we concluded our search. It was later determined on March 7, 2012 when her remains were discovered that we were within 1.3 miles from where her remains were discovered. The area that R.T. described and sketched matched perfectly and precisely to the location of P.B. remains found.

The area was by a horse trail/ranch and her remains were discovered by a runoff creek. One of my sources with the coroner's office stated directly that the tool marks found on the bones, were consistent with that of a screwdriver and having been hit in the head with that type of instrument. The suspect that R.T. had stated in the beginning of this investigation was indeed the killer. He was arrested and charged with first-degree murder, second-degree murder, and second-degree kidnapping.

R.T. was right on ALL points and was a very critical part of this investigation. The insight given from him being hundreds of miles away, without any prior knowledge whatsoever, proved to be of a very valuable stance in the fight against crime in this case.

We passed along the information gathered in our investigation, to the complete investigative team on the case before the suspect was apprehended and arrested for murder.

Thank you, Robbie Thomas, for your valuable input in assisting us with our investigation and finding the key evidence in this case that helped put things into perspective. From being hundreds of miles away and no prior knowledge of the area, circumstances, or intricate evidence already gathered, it is amazing how you work at what you do.

Thank you

(Ret) Det. Sgt. Cliff Christ,

Night Watch Commander Drug Interdiction Unit

Psychic Profiler The Real Deal

During 2007, I was contacted by Sgt. Cliff Christ, who became a friend of mine through social media. He assembled an investigative team that was looking for a lady by the name of Paige Birgfeld, from Grand Junction, Colorado. He explained to me, there were no tips or leads to go on at that time, however, there were certain items found that were of interest to the case and would I be interested in assisting them in the attempt to find more evidence, or possibly find Paige Birgfeld who was missing. It was through this contact and various phone calls back and forth that we decided it best; I do indeed assist in this case with them. The hours and days to follow, were very intriguing, very analytical and long as we all began what would be considered a very lengthy process of back and forth, with much documentation and phone calls. What you are about to read is exactly how everything played out in this investigation that has a rollercoaster affect, which will keep you glued to the storyline.

Sgt. Christ sent me photos of Paige Birgfeld, to which I began my channeling on the dynamics of this high profile case. Things, in the beginning seemed a bit off to me for the most part; however, time would prove to be the unique tool I indeed needed. I remember the many phone calls back and forth, as SJ, Sgt. Cliff Christ's wife was also part of those calls. SJ, was a first responder with the firefighters and took a very active role in this case alongside her husband, as there were many teams of investigators, searching for this beautiful missing lady. The tension and mood was set from the time of that first phone call and now, the stage was set for how important it was to get on track, and keep the information coming to the investigators.

I began with doing my automatic hand drawings, and sketches of whatever came across my mind's eye, trying to capture something of value in this case for those at the other end in Colorado. I began asking questions, to see, if I could get a feel from Sgt. Christ of anything he would release to me that might actually correspond with what I was seeing, prior to me sending it to him. Regardless, he was steadfast in not wanting to relinquish any information at this point, and was determined to have me give him the first insight of a connection that would prove to be a "hit" in this case. We tussled back and forth, with many things popping in my mind, and what I was seeing, which only made him listen more attentively without saying a word.

Part of the conversation, dealt with the insightfulness of me seeing horses and ranches, but not just any ranch or horses, no, it had to do with (what I personally never heard of before), nevertheless, was seeing, "quarter horse ranches" or signs of this about them. Details came in fast, just like a movie being played in my mind, but more comprehensive, as if, I was walking the precise way and area the perpetrator did. I could see the dried up river bed, or creek bed, and then a hole, a hole that seemed to be only half dug, or very shallow because of being hurried to do so. The area, in which this was, also came across to me as out and away from people, but easily accessible to someone who had much knowledge of this area. I felt, as if, this place was scouted out prior to, almost like being preplanned in some sense, planned out because the control factor of this psychopath wanted it this way and only this way.

Psychic Profiler The Real Deal

It seemed to me that everything was rushed, nothing left for chance as I felt. Something was of importance and this had to be done quickly in a hurried fashion, so not to be caught. I sensed the idea of looking over my shoulders continuously, in a manner of which, I was being pressured or guarded from this crime I committed, yet I wanted total control on where she would be so I could visit and visit often.

I walked in a visual of content, running through my mind's eye, something equivocal to a vengeful murderous plot, conniving, and detailed that I wanted to be caught, if that makes sense. I felt at that moment, I was actually within the mindset of a monster and the emotions that ran through me were indeed of a psychopath, who needed that control over his victim no matter what it took. I make mention to SJ that this individual we're dealing with, was someone who was of more than just an acquaintance, but more of a jilted lover. This was a crime of passion, a crime of control…it was a crime of never wanting to let go, "until death do us part!"

I began thinking to myself, what kind of sick, twisted, perverted, individual, are we dealing with here. I can actually feel everything this monster was planning, doing, and was about to do, in the post crime he had committed. I saw things that would only be fitting for a crime show of the week, or at the movies, which was so over rated, blown out of proportion, and just deviant in every meaning of the word. We had a real psycho on our hands, and one that I felt would do it again, if given that opportunity. We had to act, and act fast in this case, before someone else would fall victim to this sick individual's murderous plots.

My sketching and automatic hand drawings were all over the place, from quarter horse ranches, signs, highways, fence lines, river/creek beds, half dug holes, and the list went on and on. I envisioned the investigators actually walking the path they took, over rocks, the dried field/creek bed, and complete terrain. We discussed much over the phone throughout this investigation, which was very helpful in narrowing down the criminal mind, to which now, we we're no longer one step behind this suspect, but one ahead of him, and closing in real fast.

After establishing the fact of a certain area, and the topography of the land, those on the other end in Grand Junction, were putting their thinking caps on, trying to picture and pinpoint exactly what I was seeing. A few areas of interest matched what I was speaking of on many levels, which kept to what Law Enforcement had already investigated; however, with more detailed information now.

To me, after advising Sgt. Christ of the suspects' characteristics and profiling him, we knew he was one foot ahead of us and now it's our turn to reverse this train of thought. We came to the conclusion that someone had to make a move and encroach on the suspect's turf - which would definitely put him on notice – in order to give us a clear look at his response as we entered his workplace. This moment sunk deep within me in knowing that Sgt. Cliff Christ was about to put himself in harm's way. It was a quick plan, but a very good one that had many possibilities; which, would be perfect for us to either see his temperament, body language, or get a glance at his environment he was in.

Psychic Profiler The Real Deal

Sgt. Christ suggested he'll go into the suspects' workplace and act as a customer, or play a mechanic himself, and apply for a job while posing questions and looking for his workstation. This was going undercover in the most dangerous way; however, it proved to be a huge break for us as things started to unfold quickly, just as we suspected it to happen!

There was a part of the investigation where we discussed earlier that the suspect might become spooked and him leaving his workplace to follow the investigators vehicle. The intensity of those investigators, explaining detail by detail of what was taking place, really kept me on the edge of my seat as I envisioned the complete scenario unfolding . The heightened awareness of this monster following them down the road, and hearing the very acute conversation between the investigators over the phone, was frightening to say the least. This was a huge breakthrough, knowing that we called him out on an idea and he fell for it, showing us he was nervous that he had been made. No longer able to sit in his darkened shadows, for we made him vulnerable, playing right into our hands and this is what we wanted; a suspect showing his true colors!

As Sgt. Christ along with the investigators left the suspects work, they were immediately followed by him, which made everyone very nervous, and trying to come up with a quick exit plan. The intensity of the car chase exhilarated, as now, the investigators who were on the phone with me, explaining step by step what was occurring; finally, were able to pull a quick turn in the road, losing the suspect.

Things were really getting creepy, but we knew, we knew we had him, making him aware of our presence. It was later discovered that the direction in which the suspect traveled, was indeed the direction of where we suspected him going, to the half dug hole that had a woman's blouse discovered. This area was not close to town whatsoever; it was an area one would travel out of their way to be, and away from any people noticing anything happening. Desolate, and away from any immediate contact to population, it would serve his purpose for what he has made up in his mind.

This was an area once searched by the Sheriff's office at one point, but again, was a vast terrain that needed much more looking at. Here's where Sgt. Cliff Christ, SJ, and the investigators discovered tire tracks and footprints, as if, someone got out of their vehicle only to walk a certain distance and then stop in the middle of nowhere, to glance over at their secret hiding place. We all discussed this over the phone, finding it very odd these tracks; furthermore, who in their right mind would just pull up to this area, way out in the middle of nowhere, exit their vehicle, only to walk a few paces in one direction and then stop. It was a stop to check up on an area of interest is what it was!

We concluded that this was the suspects' tracks, as this was the direction in which he took after following the investigative team away from his workplace. During this portion of the investigation, Sgt. Christ, and his team discovered a woman's polka dot blouse near a shallow dug hole. I was later told that this is the type of clothing Paige Birgfeld wore or would have worn.

Psychic Profiler The Real Deal

Have we just discovered the first crime scene and evidence on this case, and now, we have the suspect on the move? Things began to heat up, as we knew that this monster was well aware we were on to him. Time wasn't on our side, as winter was quickly beginning and in Colorado; when it snows, it really snows, especially up in the mountain areas. We discussed this point and the field trips would have to be picked up again in the spring. We were so close, putting the heat on this guy as we just needed a bit more time, but Mother Nature had other plans.

The investigation cooled down and went quiet for a while; meanwhile, everything we had done and recorded throughout was handed over to the Law Enforcement heading up the entire investigation from Sgt. Christ. Now, we wait!

November 21ˢᵗ, 2014, a day we all have been waiting for! I get this message from SJ, and she was ecstatic to let me know right away. "It's Who You Said It Was!" She just messaged me on social media and threw a link up from a newswire. The day had come finally! The arrest of Lester Jones had happened and all the anxiety, patience, drive, and excitement, had finally come to the outcome we all knew that was going to happen.

Things flashed back in my mind, from the time Sgt. Christ asked me on the phone, if I was certain this was the guy I was seeing just before they went into his workplace for that encounter. Things like, being on the phone with SJ, discussing the path they walked towards that dried up creek bed etc.

The images that crossed my mind of that half dug hole and blouse they had found, along with the tire marks and footprints. The suspect, following them down the road in a hurried pace, knowing he had been made.

All these thoughts and feelings came rushing over me; knowing, we did the right thing, and nothing went in vain. We did this for a lady who was taken from her family, friends, and people who loved her. The gratification I guess, would be in knowing the fact, we pulled together as a team behind the scenes, wanting to put an end to this nightmare and find some type of resolution to this case.

I thank from the bottom of my heart, Detective Sgt. Cliff Christ, his wife SJ, and all those who assisted them in this investigation; for it takes many pulling together to find resolution in something like this and I'm thankful for them entrusting in me to be a part of this. God works in mysterious ways, ways we don't question, but just agree upon; because, we know it is right and just. Justice in this case, will be at the hands of God now as the trial is about to begin… August 2016!

August rolls around and I get a shout out on a text message from Det. Sgt. Christ. "Fingers Crossed!" Oh yes, it's that time and a time to celebrate as this monster gets what's coming to him. The trial lasted only a few weeks as the jury deliberated on September 3, 2016. I thought to myself, "Damn, that was fast, and they are deliberating already?" Something seemed off as Det. Sgt. Christ and I kept in contact over the course of those days. The defense was astonished at the fact there was so much surveillance on his client and other points of interest throughout the case were coming up.

Psychic Profiler The Real Deal

The anxiety to know what the hell was keeping them so long in their deliberation; the man is guilty as sin, and there was so much evidence against him. Finally, we get word the jury has reached their verdict. I waited patiently for that text message or phone call, something to come through. Come on it's killing me just waiting by the phone. Suddenly, the phone goes off and I paused to open the text message from Det. Sgt. Christ. "MISTRIAL!" I stared at the phone like a lost child looking for his mother. What the hell went wrong!? "Mistrial", this can't be I thought to myself, and texted back to the Detective. He explained to me once he found out more, he'd message me back.

Det. Sgt. Christ and I talked by phone and there is going to be a second trial for Lester Jones! A sigh of relief, knowing we had a second chance to nail this guy. All that work we did on this case, helping out, and now a second chance. Its teamwork, in the very essence of the word indeed! All those who were working behind the scenes, in the courts, everyone who gave anything at all to assist on this case knew and our team; we were ready for that guilty verdict this time.

December 27th, 2016, the day has come! The verdict is in and we wait. My phone once again, immediately after the verdict is read, I get a message with a link attached. I click it and all I see is, "Guilty!" Lester Jones was found guilty of murder in the first-degree, second-degree, and second-degree kidnapping. They nailed him! Pinned his sorry ass to the wall and threw away the key. Life without the possibility of parole!

I'm happy for the family of Paige Birgfeld in one sense after reading that message, yet, I know in my heart, it wasn't what they wanted. I know they wanted their Paige back. My heart goes out to them and I often think about this case, everything we went through all those days and nights, going over everything we found and tried to find. I guess in some refined moment of the day, I will once again find that feeling of gratitude for the fact; Lester Jones will never see the light of day outside his prison walls. To everyone who worked this case, my hats off to you all. Teamwork, it really does take teamwork.

God Bless Everyone!

(Taken From The Video Testimony Of Det. Sgt. Cliff Christ, Which Is On My Website As Testimony To This Case)

"I'm Cliff Christ. I'm a former Texas Police Sgt. With over twenty five years of Law Enforcement experience. I was contacted back some years ago by Robbie Thomas, to assist in the location of Paige Birgfeld. I found that all of Robbie Thomas's predictions and things he saw during remote viewing, to be factual, and it was job to locate the things that he had saw. Robbie was positive that the suspect in the murder was Lester Jones and predicted many things about Mr. Jones that have come true at this time. The area where the remains of Paige Birgfeld were found, he had drawn pictures of the area and we searched up to that area. Until the victims remains were found, we didn't realize we were less than a quarter of a mile from that location from our initial search.

Psychic Profiler The Real Deal

We did match some of the pictures Robbie Thomas had drawn of the area to include signs pointing to a horse farm, and they did match exactly. So, in all of my Law Enforcement and investigative experience, I have never encountered a person that could be so spot on with all the information he had given us, unless they were originally a suspect in this case. Of course, Mr. Thomas was nowhere near that location, so he couldn't have possibly known some of the things that he had given us. So I feel his abilities are one hundred percent truthful, and one hundred, one hundred, one hundred percent way above bar, as far as any other psychic remote viewer that I have ever dealt with before!"

(Ret) Det. Sgt. Cliff Christ,
Night Watch Commander Drug Interdiction Unit
Colorado

When a situation arises as in this case where assistance was needed, many people come together for the common good of helping. There were many individuals working on this case, who were on the front lines and behind the scenes, for the commonality of one thing, to help solve a heinous crime and bring justice for Paige Birgfeld and her family.

God Bless Everyone Who Helped Out In This Case
God Bless Paige Birgfeld And Her Family!

Kelsey Smith

"When my youngest daughter was a teenager in 2007, I remember getting an overwhelming, uneasiness that something dark was either around her, or that something terrible would happen to her. So, you can only imagine the horrible shock everyone felt in Overland Park, Kansas when young Kelsey Smith, who was only 18 at the time, went missing from a Target parking lot. It was the same Target I went to with my own daughter. I called my friend Laura Placeras and we both cried, praying for Kelsey. At the time, we were both managing a small internet radio program called, Full Moon Radio, and recently had interviewed a man named Robbie Thomas, who was a psychic, working with police to find missing or murdered children.

I remember Laura calling Robbie, asking if he could be of any assistance in the disappearance of Kelsey, if Laura contacted the detective on the case. He agreed, so, she called the detective, saying she had a friend who worked with Law Enforcement assisting with murder/missing person's cases. They agreed to work with him over the phone while Laura gathered as much information as she could. Laura explained to Robbie the Police were waiting for any information whatsoever that he might be able to come up with to help in this investigation. The phone conversation between Laura and Robbie lasted some time, as he filtered through what he was seeing while Laura wrote down everything.

Psychic Profiler The Real Deal

He didn't feel she was alive. He said he felt she was in a woody park area, where there was water, near a tree. He also said she was at or near the border of two Kansas. It was so sad because everyone was praying she would be found alive and this just didn't sound good. I thought he was wrong because of the border mention, but we forgot about Kansas being so close on the border of Missouri, which means there are two borders of Kansas. The information submitted was very beneficial and aided in helping Law Enforcement in their investigation as Laura did convey this to Robbie from the Detective she spoke with. They did finally catch the man who had abducted her and was a stranger to Kelsey. She was everyone's daughter at that moment and we all cried. Tape and wrapping paper that was what she needed at Target. It was a simple errand that ended up in a horrible situation where a monster took her life. It was very unselfish of Robbie as he didn't hesitate to give of himself for a little girls' sake. In the end, Robbie helped as much as he could in the time frame that was left, however, the information he did help with was ideal and spot on."

Sandy Jorgensen
Olathe, Kansas

It was one of those phone calls I dreaded, one where the person on the other end has bad news all day long. On this day, an individual I came to know through the paranormal and who became a friend, just happen to be on the other end. She was very anxious in her voice, as she blurted out many things about a young girl gone missing, and that there was no time, please help! Laura had this shakiness to her on the phone, an urgent request for help for a young lady who was abducted at a Target store. She went on about video of a truck, a guy who took this girl named Kelsey, and that she had already spoken to the Police indicating to them I might help.

I had to slow her down, just in order to get the facts of what she was trying to tell me under one long breath. Once we established the fact of the importance of this matter was, she emailed me a photo of this young girl, who was taken in the parking lot of a store in Kansas. I explained to Laura that I'd try my best in seeing what information, if at all I could obtain in regards to this abduction, and for her to write things down as we spoke over the phone. I started to explain that this individual wasn't from the area; I felt he was a stranger in this whole situation unknown to this young girl. I began giving information on two borders, which at the time, being Canadian; I truly didn't know that there was two borders for Kansas, (Kansas City, Kansas, and Kansas City, Missouri). I started seeing a park very close by, not far from where she was taken, no more than ten-fifteen minutes at most. It had water and I kept seeing a tree or behind a tree, almost like hovering around it, as if, it was a significant item to write down.

Psychic Profiler The Real Deal

I didn't feel she was with us any longer, however, you want to look for the good in anything bad, and we hurried to get as much information as we could for the detectives. At this point, there wasn't much more that came through, other than the steady feeling of hurry, hurry to that area immediately. I stressed this to Laura as she took her final notes to pass along to those waiting for the information. On that June 2, 2007, I'll never forget the horrendous, heinous crime that was committed, as Laura called me once more, giving me the news of them finding Kelsey. My heart sunk, it sunk so deep because this young girl and her family, I just couldn't get my head around it. I was lost for words and still am.

I, every once in a while, review cases I've helped out in or on shows I do. It may have only been a few minutes in assisting, but it took my heart for the rest of my life. I can't imagine her family and what they are or have gone through; it's something no one wants to have happen to them. Whenever that phone rings and it's someone asking for help for their daughter or son or loved one, I remember Kelsey and all the others I have tried helping all these years. Just looking at that beautiful Angel and I have daughters, and I too worry about them and everyone's children. These monsters out there are the reason I have taken my life, dedicating it to chasing each and every one of them down, assisting to put them where they belong, behind bars for the rest of their lives.

God Bless Kelsey and her family always!

Producer For X-Zone Radio Goes Missing!

Back in 2009, I received a peculiar request by email to call Rob McConnell from the X-Zone radio show. It only described briefly, he was in dire need of my assistance and to call as soon as possible. Normally Rob would send me emails, asking me to appear in his late night internet radio show. The phone call turned into something much more serious than expected. Apparently, a BOLO went out from the Hamilton County Sheriff's Office that an individual, who was associated to the internet show, had gone missing.

Rob filled me in that they contacted another psychic, who was at the time on a Psychic program on television for his help. It seemed through the information I was told, this psychic explained he felt Cory was shot in a hotel room in Florida area; however, couldn't visualize, or come up with enough information to place what hotel Corey was in. Rob requested I see what I could come up with and shipped me a photo of Corey while on the phone. As I went through my motions of channeling Spirit, in order to gain some sense of what truly happened to Corey, and if he was indeed shot dead in a hotel somewhere in Florida, information began to come through differently. I explained that I didn't feel he was shot whatsoever, also, that Corey wasn't dead! The conversation paused for a moment and I remember Rob's very words, "Are you sure? Because, we had a guy from a Psychic show, tell us different and he's popular!"

Psychic Profiler The Real Deal

I rolled my eyes, as I realized, popularity doesn't mean you're right, it really doesn't mean you're "Psychic" either! The show was called, The X-Zone, but sure felt like a Twilight Zone segment! I began to further on more information saying, "No, he's alive and will notify you somehow in three days of this." There continued, some doubt in what I was saying coming from Rob, as it seemed more easy to believe he was dead, rather the fact he was alive.

Anyways, I continued through the reading, "He's upset at being passed up for a promotion or something not right at the radio show! He's not in Florida, I see him in another State. "This seemed to be not what Rob was expecting and shrugged it off, thanking me in spite of already receiving information that Corey was shot and dead in a hotel somewhere in Florida!

I thought to myself at the time, "No, things just don't feel or seem right in what is being told me. It just seemed like a guess at best in hopes it would turn out to be right!" But then again, they had a guy from television that was "psychic", which means he must be right, right!?

A few days went by as I was checking my email and up pops an email from the X-Zone radio show producer, Rob McConnell.

I'll let the email speak for itself as it clearly validates everything! As well, there is a validation letter from a lady who used to help out at the X-Zone Radio Program, Dianne Laramee from the R.C.M.P. here in Canada.

Producer Goes Missing For The X Zone Radio Show

----- Original Message -----

From: Producer

To: rob thomas

Sent: Saturday, February 04, 2006 10:18 AM

Subject: 'X'Zone Radio

Dear Robbie, Sometimes I think you are an angel...I'm sorry I didn't get your reply in time, but,....It all worked out okay . I have wonderful news,... Corey's' mom just called and he is fine! He was ticked off, just like you said.....he said he didn't think anyone would even notice he was gone. Thank-you for all you have done Robbie..........we so very much appreciate it.

God Bless, Laura and Rob

Robbie,

"Upon reading that you are going to write a new book about the cases that you worked on and assist to solve, I would like to give a testimonial about the one case that I remember the most. It was in the winter, and I was helping Rob McConnell, host of the X-Zone behind the scenes with Rob Catlin with the chat lines. This night in particular, I remember that Rob McConnell had invited Robbie Thomas to be on the air.

Psychic Profiler The Real Deal

The main topic was that a person who was associated with the X-Files had gone missing. The person's name was Corey Y. During the show, I remember Rob McConnell asking you to channel Corey to which you did. You mentioned that he (Corey Y.) was still alive and wasn't dead at all.

In addition, you also mentioned that Corey Y. wasn't in Florida. In complete disbelief, I also remember Rob McConnell stating that he had been told that another psychic had told him that Corey had been shot and asked you if you were sure.

My head was spinning. Here was Rob McConnell asking for help and then basically destroying the help that he got. The feeling I had at the moment, was: "Is Rob McConnell playing you guys, but most importantly taking the easy way out by believing the other psychic?"

I was thankful; however, that Rob McConnell ask all whom were listening to the show to help find Corey Y. A couple of days later, I heard Rob McConnell state that Corey Y, had been found I smiled. Robbie, you have an amazing gift, and I have witnessed it numerous times.

With much love, respect and appreciation.

Thank You!"
Dianne Laramee
R.C.M.P. (Retired)

The Good, The Bad, The Ugly

The Ugly

When I sat down to write this chapter on everything about being a psychic profiler, much reflection has gone through my mind. I can't say, sure, it's been the greatest of achievements in my life, all rosy and bonbons, but then again; it really wouldn't be telling the entire story everyone needs to hear. "Why hold back now", I think to myself, as the entire book is totally factual with undisputed truth within its pages. No, I would be doing the wrong thing and in light of that, this is the chapter that will set aside that entire fairytale scenario people think in their minds.

The phone rings and out of desperation a family on the other end is seeking help in their loved ones' murder case. Immediately, many thoughts cross my mind as I listen to the horrific story being told to me on the other end. Once we get past the entire initial story, introduction, and the plea for help; there are a few requirements on my part I always state. Sometimes, this doesn't go over very well, nor is it accepted in a friendly manner; however, my policy of assisting, in any case, must be met. I also state within this chapter, I won't hold back on anything written, as I do believe people need to see the exact way some, and I say "some", have that acquired way of expressing their displeasure, but demand and the key word here is "demand" my time.

Psychic Profiler The Real Deal

I don't know what it is about some folks when they assume because it is a "gift" that you are to gift it to them without question or no compensation. It doesn't work like that in the real world. I look at this as two fold really, one being, folks really don't understand or have the knowledge of what really goes on in cases that a Psychic Profiler assists with. Second, I believe they feel that, if it doesn't take much of your time and effort, why should anyone afford this profession or your time. I stand by my feelings this way. If you hire a lawyer, who is specialized in what he does, you pay his fee. If you hire a private detective, who specializes in what he does, you pay his fee. Police, they are already on the job being paid. A specialist in medicine charges differently than that of a family physician and that leaves me. I specialize in something totally different than that mentioned above; therefore, anyone who can't do what I do, makes this a specialized field of work I work in. When it involves taking up long periods of time, countless hours and puts my life at risk for strangers, it truly is priceless.

The flip side of this coin? How much to charge and what is appropriate. It's entirely different in each case that's presented to me. Every case is different in variables, which means it could entail me traveling far distances for days at a time, with hundreds of hours being logged. Or, it has happened many times as well, where I sit on the phone, looking at a photograph of a baby, or a missing elderly lady, and within minutes the case has been solved. How do you put a price on that you might ask? Easy, it is assessed by me as a case, regardless of time and effort.

See, if it weren't for calling me, asking me for my assistance, this would have never found its resolution or a path to a resolution in the end. Even though I do what I do, it's still me taking my valuable time doing it. There is no price anyone can put on that, it's priceless; however, because it was me and my "gift", I reserve the right to charge whatever it is I ask! I pull no punches and call it like it is, I'm a straight shooter when it comes to this profession, and yes, it is a profession that is quickly being recognized!

Some might sour at these statements; however, once again, everything in life has a price, especially being in such demand. One must realize as well, this has become a twenty-four hour, seven days a week roller coaster ride. My life doesn't stop for anyone, nor would I expect anyone to do the same for me. In light of everything, I understand people really don't know the functionality of doing what I do, nor do they completely comprehend the risk factor my life takes. I don't just look at my life, I look at my family, friends and everyone I'm associated to. I don't write this to be scornful or resentful in any respect, I write this chapter to enlighten and bring some sense of realization of the matter. For the most part, when you sit and think of it, situations that arise never come with instructions; therefore, there must be some foundation in place to guide in the anticipation of getting that call. Professionalism in any occupation, if you will, has a distinction of separation in our society, which gives everyone the understanding just what it is a person does. This is only one part of the "Ugly" in the life of me.

The Bad!

When we talk about the bad, we get into the scenarios of families desire to make a spectacle at times of cases. This I can't and still to this day, don't understand. When I'm on a case, working with other professionals in the Law Enforcement, things always seem to take many twists and turns with families at times. Not all, just some, but it is a large amount of "some" that do this.

It becomes glorified news frenzy, as the media feasts on the publicity of a high profile psychic medium, which has traveled from far, assisting Law Enforcement and this creates havoc. It's happened to me many times and currently going through this. I don't know what it is about notifying every reality television show about crime, to boast or publicize their family's case while it's being investigated. I get the expressions of, "we want it to be in the public's eye!"

My answer to that is always the same, why on earth would you want the public to know detailed information, or what's going on at the time? It will only inhibit many individuals who just want to poke their noses into something they have no right, or have no qualifying information that is tangible. It just doesn't make sense! Furthermore, you're letting those who are responsible, know we are on to them or investigating certain elements of the case. They get to know our timeline, factors, who's been brought in on the case, and for what, for ratings on some two bit reality show or news headline in the paper!? This type of thing is for the end, when everything has been solved.

Just because things aren't moving fast enough, or to the family's liking, they jump the gun so-to-speak, which only really hinders the investigation on many levels.I have and had, producers from many crimes shows from Los Angeles to New York, calling my office or emailing me, wanting, no…no, let me rephrase that, "demanding", yes that it, to see evidence I have or gained with Law Enforcement, so they can make a show out of it. Oh, I had one major network want to fly me out to a case we got a conviction on for double homicide, just to show them where the body would be, before the police finished their investigation in finding it. How ludicrous is that!?

My strong opinion and suggestion to any family going through a loved one's murder case being investigated, patience! Yes, patience is the key in any investigation, be it one month, one year, or ten. Murder has no statute of limitations and sometimes cases wrap up in days, weeks and years, but it takes strength within, the knowledge of understanding, time, and professionalism. Going to a television show, or the newspaper or magazine doesn't help anything whatsoever. They might think it does, but in the end, when everything falls apart, the finger pointing starts. Oh yes, the finger pointing! Take it from me, if things don't go the way they thought it should; outside of the normal practice of investigation, and they've taken matters into their own hands, which will always ends up being a disaster in the making. Finger pointing starts and the blaming game begins.

Psychic Profiler The Real Deal

Law Enforcement gets plenty of this and I've been brought in on cases as such, but when you fact check the intentions from the families at times, what they've done, they have no one to blame but themselves. Truth hurts sometimes, but it's the truth! Outside interference is just what is it…interference! I totally understand and get it! Families want productive situations and the urgency to have that is precedent to them. I know from experience, day in, day out, they live the horrors of their loved one's case and this is terrible. My heart goes out to each family I come to know, but there is a separation of coming to know them and being able to assist them in the proper fashion.

Setting aside feelings, thoughts and for the most part, them, will only allow a better outcome in the end because of staying focused on the task at hand. "Celebritizing" a case, isn't where it's at whatsoever, there is a time for that, but to put the horse before the cart, we're only cutting off our nose to spite our face. This issue becomes emotions, and we all know emotions often more times than enough, lead the way in every scenario in life. I've come to learn over the vast many years, once we establish that pillar of understanding, following it can be tested at times; however, it must be adhered to. It will only benefit the case in the end and bring about a better resolution and closure for Law Enforcement and the Psychic Profiler.

The Good

This part I love! From everything you just read above, this is what it should be. Folks get it, they truly do, and they deserve the better part of the investigation on their case. When you have complete cooperation from all family members, and they entrust their case with you, things work smoothly for the most part. I've walked in on cases, speaking with Law Enforcement in meetings and headed out to the death scenes to gather vital information that I can render. See, the biggest component of a case, is time, but it has to be utilized in the proper context of that meaning.

We have to establish "boundaries", which I always do on any case I get called in on. I'm not there to waste anyone's valuable time and effort; I'm there to find resolve or a solution to move cases forward. This is very vital to which is clearly seen in the approach I take on the level with Law Enforcement. Once the foothold of what is established by the leading Detective on a case, we banter back and forth my envisioned impressions that match what is already known in the case at hand, and thus, we move forward to things that are needed to pursue more information adding it to the case.

Psychic Profiler The Real Deal

Resolution only comes from feasible and tangible assets that can be utilized in a case. Law Enforcement utilizes everything they have that revolves around any case to their advantage allowing them to get that one clue or piece of evidence to make a turn in a case or to actually solve it right out. The best part of a case I like is when everything runs smoothly. Of course that is what anyone would want right, but even though there might be some snags along the way, as long as none of the "Ugly or Bad" has entered the picture, things always turn out for the better.

I have a saying… "Putting Families First & Criminals Where They Belong!"

Just my two cents worth and I hope it was valuable information for you… God Bless

Social Media And Your Children

Over the years I've been called by many families about their children who go missing, and then, finding out afterward that social media was the basis for this occurrence to take place. Yes, it is a problem and yes, as parents, we need to be vigil because of the vast social media outlets kids have at their fingertips. I'm sitting in my office as I write this out while Dr. Phil is playing on the television. I'm watching this father's plight for educating the public on his daughter's death because of the use of social media and the contact with a pedophile. The harsh reality of life is there are predators out there all over social media, lurking like a carnivorous wild animal, waiting to pounce on its prey when it sees an opportunity.

The key is to get involved in your child's life, as much as possible, if that means becoming more than mom and dad, and becoming that friend, do it! Social media is not a face friendly application when it comes to your child's life. Manipulators sit patiently by, waiting for the next victim to cross their screens in places like KIK, Twitter, Facebook, SnapChat, MySpace, or many others platforms out there.

The world is made of many evil people unfortunately and I've personally been on the front lines with families who have been or seen this evil. It breaks my heart every time when I'm contacted by a devastated father, or mother that their child has been abducted or murdered. There is no pain in this world that can describe what they go through, but you can hear it in their voice and feel it in their words.

Psychic Profiler The Real Deal

That is all that's left is the voice of the mother or father, who are torn deeper than ever, empty within and you know there is absolutely nothing you can do to give them their baby back. The hollowed cries from their souls echo through the phone or in person, as I've sat with many families, and it just rips you apart seeing them in their pain.

If there's anything at all that makes any sense whatsoever in what I've tried to convey in this message, please speak to your children and don't be afraid to be as open and close to them as you can. Be on their social media's, be involved and don't just dismiss it as it's only Facebook, or Twitter, KIK, Myspace or any social media. Love your children more than enough, more than just it's your child, love them as they are YOUR LIFE!

Education is the key, use it! And GOD FORBID, anything terrible happens to you who are reading this now. Life is always changing, faster at times than we care to see it, but we can be on top of things just as quick and keep our children safe!

Stay Vigilant and Persistent
God Bless You All!

Final Words

They Called, I Answered That Call
Without Hesitation Or Demand!

Thank you, everyone who has taken the time to read Psychic Profiler – The Real Deal, True Crime Cases Vol. 1. Over the many years of answering the call, there is one thing in life I have come to realize, and that is by answering those calls; together, we give hope and faith to those who are seeking it. It's in giving unselfishly to those who reach out making that call that I have learned it is the right thing to do and that is to help. This, in its entirety is something no one can condemn or speak out against as it is just. It truly does take a village to raise a child, for we are all children of God.

Thank you!
God Bless…

Other Books By Robbie Thomas

www.robbiethomas.net

Made in the USA
Columbia, SC
17 February 2018